Five Minutes To

Inspired

Action

and

Results

For Professionals

By
Rachelle Huddleston

Copyright © 2021 by Rachelle Huddleston. All rights reserved.

No part of this book may be reproduced in any form or by an electronic or mechanical means, including information storage and retrieval systems, without written persmission from the author, except for the use of brief quotations in a book review.

ISBN: 979-8-5223-5930-0

*With special thanks to those
who have served as my coach in this life.*

Foreword

It was 2011 when I first met Rachelle Huddleston while participating in a community-based leadership development program. I found her to be engaging and someone who challenged the class to push themselves outside each of our own "comfort zones". After completion of the year-long course, I knew she could help me in developing and building-out my financial advising practice so I began working with her one-on-one.

I had been working as a financial advisor for 4 years at that point and had decent success growing the practice, attracting clients, and growing revenues, but I was running myself ragged and knew in my heart that if

I didn't figure out a way to get a better grip on where and how I wanted my practice to evolve, I'd find myself unhappy and burnt out. Eight years later, I continue working with Coach Rachelle. When I met Rachelle, my gross production was in the low-to-mid-6 figures. Now, I'm in the top 10% of the firm's producers, my client experience indicator score is in the top 10%, and I'd say, judging by conversations with many of my colleagues, my inner-peace and joy in my career is in the top 10% as well.

I credit Coach Rachelle with so much of this success. She continually challenges me to think outside the box when I might be stuck in the box. She encourages me to always stay true to my inner-wisdom when the world is pushing me in places I know just won't fit with my dreams and goals for my life long-term.

In this book, Rachelle shares a weekly challenge to help achieve better alignment with where you want to go in both your professional and personal life. Let's be honest, if you aren't filled with peace and joy personally, it's going to be hard to get your dreams and goals fully optimized. Life throws us curve balls all the time, but staying focused on the long-term vision and dreams you have for yourself will, in my opinion, help you ultimately achieve those goals.

So start here, open the pages ahead with an open mind, and a willingness for Coach Rachelle to help you find a path ahead that brings your life into greater alignment, with more joy and peace, and where you fully unlock your inner-potential. I know you'll be glad you did!

Kevin Makalous,
Certified Financial Planner

A journey of a thousand miles begins with a single step.
- Lao Tzu

Table of Contents

Introduction 1
    Creating Inspired Action 4
    Mission, Vision and Values 7
    A Simple Tool to Assess Your Life Satisfaction 9
    Create a Vision of Your Success 12
    Your Top Values 15
    Instructions 17
    Your Personal Values 19

Inspired Achievement 24
    A Daily Action Pack 27
    Create a Schedule that Works! 30
    Has Your Cheese Moved? 33
    Putting A Stake in the Ground 36
    The Slight Edge 39
    Aim Your Arrow at Your Target! 42
    The Strength of Your Arrow 45
    Overcoming Obstacles to Achievement 48
    Making SMART Goals SPICY! 52
    "Being" To Get Results 55
    Accountability as a Power Tool 58
    One Thing 61

Lean In to Communication and Leadership 65
    A Quick Tip for Improving Relationships 67

Courageous Conversations 70
Positive Moments of Truth 74
The Law of Recency: What have you done for me LATELY?
.... 77
The Only Way to Lead 80
Try Not! 83
Fit not Fault 86
The Extra Degree 89
Taking Flight 92

Authentic You 96
An Infusion of Joy 99
Care for Your Heart! 102
The Gift of the Life You Desire 105
Small Kindnesses 108
Surfing the Waves of Change 110
A New Day and a True You! 113
Living Your strengths 116
Being Who You Are 119
Get Your Needs Met 122
It's Already In You! 126
"You are Here" - Right Where You Need to Be 129

A Winning Mindset 133
Bring It into Focus 135
Getting a Handle on "No" 138
Learning the Lesson To Advance 142
Opening Up Options 145

Releasing the Outcome 148
Rewrite Your Story! 151
The Value of the Stinky Stuff 154
What You Resist Will Persist 157
The Re-think Process 161
Reset Your Default 164
Recharge in 59 seconds! 167
Lighten Your Luggage! 170
Just Business 173
Are You At Your Cruising Altitude? 176
Honoring the Duck that Lays the Golden Eggs 179
Live Like You Mean It 182
Lucky 13 185
Practice Makes Perfect 188
What's in Your Bucket? 191

Comfort and Courage for the Soul 194

References 196

ASK! 199

Your Invitation to Inspired Action and Results 201

About Rachelle 202

Introduction

❖

Each year we are given the gift of 52 weeks to create what we want for our lives. Yet many find themselves unable to hurdle the challenges and sustain movement towards the goal, frequently at odds with our own schedules, relationships and ultimately, ourselves. Some call it struggle – feeling as if we are in a fight to create the successful life we're working so hard to achieve.

Others accept struggle as the status quo – the price of success.

In my work with successful individuals, the value of having an internal sense of peace - that is, the calm that comes from the satisfaction of a day well lived and a job well done, cannot be overrated. Releasing the struggle and gaining a sense of peace and internal satisfaction in your profession is, simply put, priceless.

Powerful Question: A year from now, what do you want your life to look like?

This book is a self-coaching tool that will help guide you to answers that energize your momentum, strategies that help you move forward powerfully, and interactive exercises to create greater achievement and satisfaction both professionally and personally. The collection of 52 coaching insights are designed for your weekly reflection and action, along with a weekly accountability tool taking you through a year of inspired achievement. Ultimately, you will discover what inspires your action and gets your results!

Invest 5 minutes

You are worth the investment! Knowing that your life is demanding, the tips are brief, including a request for your personalized action.

Take Action!

We use to say that "knowledge is power." But now knowledge is just an internet search away. Knowledge, in and of itself, is no longer power. There is a need to take the knowledge and apply it in a meaningful way. With this in mind, each coaching tip provides a valuable insight, and invites you to create your own personal application. Based on your personal application, you decide what action you will take to strengthen your satisfaction and your results both in your life and career. Each tip asks for the investment of your response. Use your action plan to move powerfully into your day and your week. It is my hope that you are inspired to take action that makes good sense for your life, and that those actions get you the results and the satisfaction you really want. Your desired life is strengthened by living in alignment with your best self, honoring what is most important to you and to those you love.

Maximize your reading

With each coaching challenge, you will find a corresponding **_Week In Action page_** to track your progress and gain self-accountability to daily action. Each day, jot down your action, record your progress and make adjustments as needed for the following day. This provides a simple guide to stay on track, and a way to look back over the year at a glance to see what action you have taken to create more of the life you truly wanted. Should you decide that an accountability partner would help create the results you really want, contact me for further information on the services available for you.

Creating Inspired Action

Inspired action is action that is aligned with your core values and personal mission. This type of action engages your strengths and interests in a way that energize you as well as others who are impacted by your work and your life. When you are taking action that is in alignment with your core values and your personal mission, the action is strengthened by the fact that it intuitively makes sense and feels right to you. That personal alignment strengthens your presence and becomes an attractor to those who are looking for the service and products you provide.

I like to compare it to your vehicle's alignment. A car will continue to run even if it is out of alignment. However, the vehicle will start to pull hard to one side, require much more effort to steer, and make it impossible to feel at ease while driving. If le" out of alignment, the warning signs get more intense, and the car experiences other problems, like an annoying vibration and tires wearing unevenly, leading to more costly repairs, and decreasing any chance of truly enjoying the ride.

On the other hand, when your car is in alignment, it runs smoothly and steers with very little effort. Your focus and energy are freed up to give attention to other things that need it. When living in personal alignment with core values and a personal mission, your actions become an expression of your personal mission and values. You have a compelling reason to take that action, feeling awake and alive, knowing you are moving forward in a way that honors who you really are in all of your endeavors.

Inspired action also takes place when we choose to infuse our lives with more of that which inspires us. If you value connection and community involvement, create a life that integrates those values. It may be involvement in a service organization that rehabs homes for the elderly, or helping with a youth group at church. It really depends on your values, your mission, and the specific gifts and interests that are uniquely yours. If you value adventure, infuse more of that in your work and in your life.

For me, my mission is to support others on a path to their unique greatness. When I am coaching others to move fully into their potential, I am in alignment with my mission. It energizes me to do this work because it fuels my mission.

It isn't always the work itself, but the reason or inspiration behind the work that makes the difference. Author and inspirational speaker Simon Sinek calls it your "Why"[1]. It's why you do what you do. As a financial advisor, it may not be inspiring if you feel you have to sell your services. However, if you fully embrace the reason you are doing this work – your own mission, you become more Confident and assured when sharing what you do.

For instance, if your personal mission is to help others succeed in life, and you value education as a way to achieve that, you may choose to specialize in helping families secure college

Inspired Action and Results

funding for their children and grandchildren. Because your mission is to help others succeed, and you value education, you become aligned with a purpose for the work you are doing. You can then Confidently share this mission with those you meet. Your particular area-of-focus (ensuring families have full funding for college tuition) will likely have you connecting with families who have young children, or older adults who want to help with their grandchildren's educational future. Does this mean that all of your clients will have this goal? Probably not all of them, however it will differentiate you from other advisors. Your unique area of specialization will attract those particular individuals, and make it easy for others to recognize appropriate referrals for you.

Inside you will find a personal values exercise (page 21). Invest the time to determine your core values and notice opportunities to honor them in the work you are doing each day. Living in alignment with your values creates a sense of power and inner peace that will not only be felt by you, it will also be recognized by others in the work you do and the life you live.

As you peruse the coaching tip titles, you can read through the tips in a traditional linear fashion from start to finish, or feel free to choose one tip each week that draws your attention and answer the thought provoking questions. Each tip offers new insight and perspective, and asks for your action. You'll also find a weekly action journal next to each tip to keep you moving throughout the week. Book mark your tip and return to it each day that week. Jot down your progress, hurdles and adjustments to stay focused on accomplishing what it is you really want to do.

It's your life. Enjoy the journey!

Mission, Vision and Values

A significant amount of time and energy is invested in developing a company's mission statement and core values. People make careers of helping others write a mission statement and clarify the company values. Yet if you ask most people, they cannot clearly state their company's mission or values. And it is rare to meet individuals who have considered their own personal mission, vision and values statements.

Knowing these concepts, and taking time to determine them for yourself are key to moving forward powerfully and experiencing personal fulfillment. Below are definitions for a personal mission, vision and values.

Mission – A brief statement that encapsulates your reason for existing - why you are here.

Vision – A mental picture of your ideal life when you are fully engaged and achieving what you are here to do.

Values – The core principles that guide and direct you. You are at your best when you uphold them in the life you live and the work you do.

Inspired Action and Results

When you are making professional and life decisions, knowing your personal mission, vision and values will clarify what options are the best fit for you, and which ones would actually weaken your position in life. For instance, if you value time with your family, it would be difficult to choose a career that required you to be out of town for long periods of time, or demanded late hours that kept you away from home each night until after your family was already asleep.

The invitation is this: Create your life in such a way that you are living your mission, honoring your values and moving powerfully towards your ideal vision for your career and your life. It's a way of living, and a practice, rather than a one-time endeavor.

The pages ahead will assist you in developing your life so it works well for you, and those you care about.

A Simple Tool to Assess Your Life Satisfaction

───────◆───────

How satisfied are you with the life you have created? It's a big question and it's a question about your life; the one and only, precious and amazing, beautiful, adventure-of-a-life that you've been gifted. In my view, you are well worth taking the time to reflect on this question and give yourself your best answer.

The Life Satisfaction Wheel is designed to identify your current satisfaction level in eight major areas of life. The simplicity of the circle design makes it easy to see where life is going well, and where it is out of balance.

Take some time to determine your current satisfaction level in the areas listed. If you have other areas you would like to rate, you can "slice the pie" into additional pieces and personalize your areas.

Instructions:

For each area, ask yourself, "On a scale from 1 – 10 (with 10 being the ideal) how satisfied am I with this area of my life?" Don't over-think it. Just go with your gut response.

___Physical Environment

___Career

___Finances

___Health/Self care

___Friends/Other Relationships

___Family

___Personal Development/Spiritual

___Leisure and Hobbies

After rating all of the areas, color in each segment of the wheel to reflect your numerical level of satisfaction, with "1" being a very low level of satisfaction, and "10" being ideal in that particular area.

Once you are clear about your current level of satisfaction, envision what each area of your life would look like if you were living it at a 10. Create the vision and write it down. Then choose an area to begin redesigning to increase your satisfaction. I encourage people to start with the area that has your attention and seems appealing to redesign. The goal is to redesign this area so that you are fully satisfied with your life. Play with it. Consider inviting a friend or spouse to join you in the redesign process. It's your life. You get to create it.

Introduction

Wheel of Life

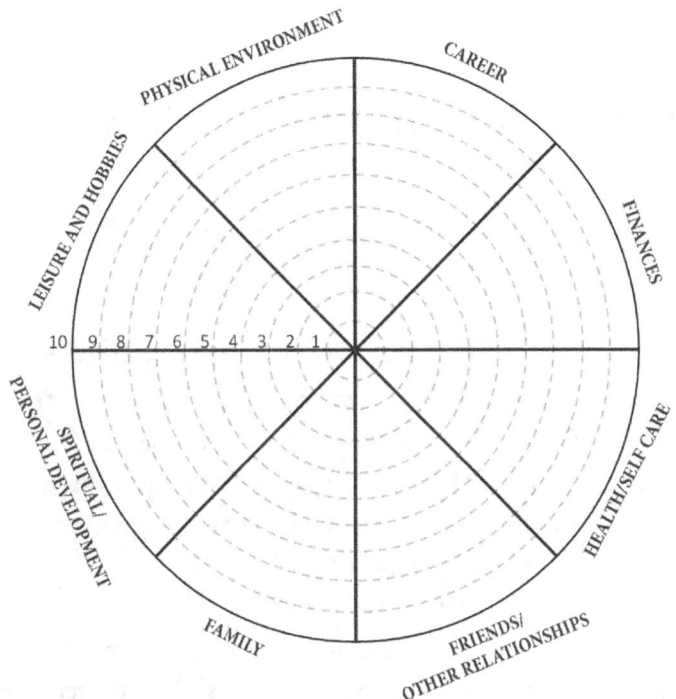

Using the satisfaction rating numbers you completed on page 10, color each section of your life wheel to the corresponding number that indicates your level of your satisfaction in each area. Each area will have its own unique level of satisfaction.

What do you notice?

What area would you like to take action to strengthen your satisfaction?

What would be your next step to strengthen your satisfaction in that area?

Let's move forward starting today!

Inspired Action and Results

Create a Vision of Your Success

―――――♦―――――

What does success look like to you? When you are achieving the professional and personal goals you've set for yourself, what will your life look like? When getting ready to take a vacation, we take the time to consider what we want from the trip. Some prefer the action of amusement parks or the energy of big cities and live theater, while others want to feel the sand beneath their feet and hear the sound of seagulls above the roar of ocean waves hitting the shore. Getting a mental picture of what your success looks like and what your life will look like when you are experiencing that success will help you make decisions and design action that creates movement towards your preferred destination. Without clarity of what you want, it's easy to get sidetracked and end up in a life that does not look like the one you want. Design your life so it is attractive to you and it aligns with what is most important to you.

Consider the following questions and jot down what success looks like for you.

- What does it look like when it's going really well?

- What do you want to be accomplishing in 5 years?
- What will your income be?
- How many hours will you work each day?
- How many days will you work each week?
- What does your family time look like?
- Will you travel for work?
- Will you have extended vacations with friends or family?
- Will you donate to special causes or volunteer time to help others?
- What emotions will you experience when you are living your vision?

What elements are important in your success?

Use the next page to write your vision for your success. You can then create intentional activities to achieve your vision. Taking daily action will support you in getting there. This can also be a valuable team or family activity to engage everyone in creating the vision. In the Inspired Achievement chapter you will find specific tips to propel you towards your vision. Read on and get ready to move into action!

Inspired Action and Results

YOUR VISION

Introduction

Your Top Values

───────♦───────

Values serve as an internal guide. When we are living in a way that honors and expresses them, we experience a greater sense of peace and satisfaction, resting in the knowledge that we are holding in high esteem that which is most important to us. When we are unaware of our true values, it becomes easier to make choices that are out of alignment with who we really are on the inside, leading to increased internal stress that plays out in many forms.

Each of us values different things. This exercise is a way to discover that there are many things/concepts/ideals that can be considered a value. They are neither right nor wrong. They just *are*. By becoming aware of your top values, you can make conscious decisions about how you want to honor your values in all areas of your life.

For instance, if you value time with your family, it is important to set limits and plan events that prioritize time with family. When you know your values, you can better honor them, and create a life that feels more authentic by honoring them. Authentic living leads to a greater sense of internal peace, and

Inspired Action and Results

tends to attract others who are a good fit for your life. When those who aren't a good fit for your life show up, it is easier to notice this and set limits that support your continued authentic presence both professionally and personally.

Introduction

Instructions

———◆———

Identifying your values involves some self-reflection. Give yourself time and space to consider which of these values are truly important to you. Notice your reaction to the various words and see what speaks deeply to you.

1. Read through the list of values first. Notice which ones stand out to you as important, and which ones do not really speak strongly about you.

2. Now read through them again and:

Put a "1" next to all of the values that are VERY IMPORTANT to you. Put a "2" next all of the values that are FAIRLY IMPORTANT to you. Put a "3" next to all of the value that are not as important to you.

Re-read all of your "1's" and decide which of the values are your Top 4. Circle the Top 4 and fill them on the following page.

It can be challenging to narrow the most important values down to 4. You will likely have identified a larger number of values that are a "1" for you. When you choose your Top 4, it doesn't mean that the others aren't important. It just means that those four are essential for you to honor to be at your personal best. Over time, you may want to work through the exercise again and see if you discover something new about yourself and your values.

My Top 4 Values

1.

2.

3.

4.

One action you will take this week to fully honor your values:

_____
_____
_____
_____

Your Personal Values

---◆---

Rate each value below as:

1 – Most important to me (or)

2 – Pretty important to me (or)

3 – Not as important to me

Re-read your "1's" and circle the Top four (4) that resonate deeply with you.

_____ Achievement

_____ Advancement and promotion

_____ Adventure

_____ Affection (love and caring)

_____ Arts

_____ Beauty

_____ Challenging problems

_____ Change and variety

_____ Close relationships

Inspired Action and Results

_____ Community

_____ Competence

_____ Competition

_____ Cooperation

_____ Country

_____ Creativity

_____ Decisiveness

_____ Democracy

_____ Ecological awareness

_____ Economic security

_____ Effectiveness

_____ Efficiency

_____ Ethical practice

_____ Excellence

_____ Excitement

_____ Fame

_____ Fast living

_____ Financial gain

_____ Friendships

_____ Growth

_____ Having a family

_____ Helping other people

_____ Helping society

_____ Honesty

_____ Independence

Introduction

_____ Influencing others
_____ Inner harmony
_____ Integrity
_____ Intellectual status
_____ Involvement
_____ Job tranquility
_____ Knowledge
_____ Leadership
_____ Location
_____ Loyalty
_____ Market position
_____ Meaningful work
_____ Merit
_____ Money
_____ Nature
_____ Being with people who are open, honest
_____ Order (tranquility, stability, conformity)
_____ Personal development
_____ Freedom
_____ Physical challenge
_____ Pleasure
_____ Power and authority
_____ Privacy
_____ Public service
_____ Purity

Inspired Action and Results

_____ Quality of what I take part in

_____ Recognition (respect from others, status)

_____ Religion

_____ Reputation

_____ Responsibility and accountability

_____ Security

_____ Self-respect

_____ Serenity

_____ Sophistication

_____ Stability

_____ Status

_____ Supervising others

_____ Time freedom

_____ Truth

_____ Wealth

_____ Wisdom

_____ Work under pressure

_____ Work with others

_____ Working alone

Once you have identified your Top 4 Values, go back to page 18 and fill them in. Making life and career decisions that honor these values will provide a sense of internal peace and confidence, knowing that you are living in a way that aligns with what is most important to you.

Introduction

*Whatever you can do or dream you can, begin it now.
Boldness has genius, power and magic in it.*

Goethe

Inspired Achievement

―――――♦―――――

Truly authentic and desirable goals can be the most motivating force in our lives. They bring individuals together to accomplish things we could not imagine doing alone. They challenge us, reveal us, and call forth our best selves. They inspire us to attempt things we would otherwise think unimaginable. Goals dare us to dream. They call us to overcome.

Often times our goals aren't energizing because we haven't connected with them in a way that energizes us, or we make concerted effort to achieve them without the systems and support needed for success to be sustainable. Aligning goals with a personal purpose and moving towards a clearly defined future gives us energy and resolve. Yet even with that, we may start to drift, feeling alone and wondering if achievement really matters, or if we will ever be able to accomplish the big, glorious goal we set out to make happen.

In the following pages you will find ways to strengthen your goals, and create your desired outcomes. Make a SMART goal SPICY. Use a new power tool. Align your arrow so it hits the target, and more. Read on and discover new ways to your inspired achievement!

The pages ahead are coaching tips designed as weekly inspiration, accountability and action.

Choose a new insight tip weekly – you can move through them in the order that they are presented in the book, or you can review the titles in the Table of Contents to find inspiration that matches your current interest.

Below are the four overarching areas, each offering multiple weekly insights for you to explore:

Inspired Achievement focuses on ways to set and achieve your goals.

Lean into Communication and Leadership provides new strategies for influencing, leading and connecting positively with others.

Authentic You invites you to experience joy and practice self-care to sustain your success.

A Winning Mindset challenges you to re-think situations and see in ways that promote growth, adaptability and ultimately your results.

This is Five Minutes to Inspired Action and Success!

Set your timer for 5 minutes daily! Choose a new tip each week and engage in the interactive exercises. Track your progress with the tracking tool provided with each weekly inspiration. Take action, eliminate hurdles and notice your progress!

Inspired Action and Results

If you would like to discuss your journey and your goals, contact me at CoachRachelle.com for a complimentary conversation to support your success.

The greatest thing in this world is not so much where we are, but in what direction we are moving. - Oliver Wendell Holmes

Keep moving in the direction of your dreams! - Rachelle Huddleston

A Daily Action Pack

A daily action pack is 2-4 intentional actions you identify and complete daily to keep you focused and moving forward powerfully. Whatever you want to accomplish today, put it in writing and do it! These actions are often related to your goals for the year, and can also be designed to handle the small things you need to get accomplished. Examples for a daily action pack:

My Daily Action Pack for Monday:

1. Meet with the team to set up accountability in our top area of focus

2. Clarify with spouse/partner my need for an hour of alone time in the evening

3. Call my colleague to thank them for the discussion and the advice

Some considerations:

- It takes less than two minutes to create the daily action pack.

Inspired Action and Results

- Keep your actions specific and attainable.
- Jot actions down or send yourself an electronic reminder to complete your action pack.
- Enjoy knowing you completed what you set out to do each day!

My Daily Action Pack for today:

1.
2.
3.
4.

Inspired Achievement

The Week in Action

Monday
Action Taken:

Hurdles Encountered:

The Plan to Move Forward Tomorrow:

Tuesday
Action Taken:

Hurdles Encountered:

The Plan to Move Forward Tomorrow:

Wednesday
Action Taken:

Hurdles Encountered:

The Plan to Move Forward Tomorrow:

Thursday
Action Taken:

Hurdles Encountered:

The Plan to Move Forward Tomorrow:

Friday
Action Taken:

Hurdles Encountered:

The Plan to Move Forward Tomorrow:

When taking action, author Brian Tracy suggests that you *eat that frog!* Do the thing that is most challenging first. Then you can focus on other things.

Create a Schedule that Works!

Ever felt like your schedule had control of you, rather than creating your schedule so that you could actually enjoy your day? Here are some "symptoms" that your schedule may be taking on a life of its own.

- You're frequently heard voicing concerns due to your many scheduled duties...
- You feel trapped by the tightness of your schedule...
- You see yourself as a victim of your schedule...
- You want to cancel everything & start over with a clean schedule...
- You begin resenting the schedule & those who are filling it...

If this is your experience, it may be time to review and renegotiate your commitments. Yes, even if you have to squeeze it into the schedule!

Eliminate, delegate or reduce.

Consider adding resources to reduce your commitments. For instance, if you drive your child to school and soccer practice daily, consider a car pool to reduce your duties as the "parent-taxi."

If you have extra-curricular meetings most evenings, turn in a resignation, or make a plan to reduce your commitments.

Stop agreeing to do more. You can still consider opportunities, however consider new commitments and opportunities after a certain amount of time - a month, or even a year!

Get real with why you have agreed to be so busy, and then debate the truth you have been telling yourself. For instance, the parent-taxi may be thinking that "if I don't do this, I am not a good parent." Is that really true? And how is that thinking serving you? What could you tell yourself instead?

This is your life! Challenge the thinking and begin to create space for the things you truly need to be your best self.

ACTION

One thing I will do (or undo) to create a new, spacious feel to my schedule:

_____
_____
_____
_____
_____

Inspired Action and Results

The Week in Action

Monday
Action Taken:

Hurdles Encountered:

The Plan to Move Forward Tomorrow:

Tuesday
Action Taken:

Hurdles Encountered:

The Plan to Move Forward Tomorrow:

Wednesday
Action Taken:

Hurdles Encountered:

The Plan to Move Forward Tomorrow:

Thursday
Action Taken:

Hurdles Encountered:

The Plan to Move Forward Tomorrow:

Friday
Action Taken:

Hurdles Encountered:

The Plan to Move Forward Tomorrow:

Schedule some weekly thinking time in your calendar. This new spaciousness will provide time to reflect, strategize and make new plans!

Has Your Cheese Moved?

———————◆———————

In a jewel of a book entitled, *"Who Moved My Cheese?"*[3] we follow a group of mice who were deliriously happy after finding a huge room of cheese, and each day they would return to the room to feast, socialize and celebrate, until the cheese began to dwindle away.

Some of the mice moved on to look for new cheese before the cheese ran out completely, but many continued to return to the same room, hoping against hope that they would find more cheese in their now-depleted cheese room. Many became hungry and anxious because each day they returned only to find the same problem - no cheese, leading to needs not being filled and the accompanying anxiety about the situation.

How about your career and your life? Is there an area where you continue to return to the same place (or people), hoping to be fulfilled, but each time you leave feeling more depleted? You may be so comfortable going back to the familiar cheese room that even when it no longer meets your needs, it's hard to see how it is depleting you.

Inspired Action and Results

The "cheese room" could be your team, a significant relationship, your social circle, a big client, or a habit that no longer serves you.

THE CHALLENGE

Identify one thing that is depleting you:

_____
_____
_____
_____

Look at this one thing over the week and consider the options that may better serve you. Pick an option and try it out. You can always return to the old cheese room if you want!

One option that may work better and I will try it out this week:

_____
_____
_____
_____

Here's to taking a risk and discovering new cheese!

Inspired Achievement

The Week in Action

Monday
Action Taken:

Hurdles Encountered:

The Plan to Move Forward Tomorrow:

Tuesday
Action Taken:

Hurdles Encountered:

The Plan to Move Forward Tomorrow:

Wednesday
Action Taken:

Hurdles Encountered:

The Plan to Move Forward Tomorrow:

Thursday
Action Taken:

Hurdles Encountered:

The Plan to Move Forward Tomorrow:

Friday
Action Taken:

Hurdles Encountered:

The Plan to Move Forward Tomorrow:

> One does not discover new lands without consenting to lose sight of the shore. -Andre Gide

Putting A Stake in the Ground

When putting a tent up, we make sure it stays up by staking it down. Each time you hammer a stake in the ground, you insure the results you expect. A firm stake in the ground will keep the tent strong even in the midst of wind, rain and other challenging elements.

Apply this to your career. What is it you want, that you haven't yet accomplished?

This week I want to encourage you to put your stake in the ground:

1. Declare what it is you want to do. Stating what you want is the beginning of making it happen.

2. Commit to your next step by stating your goal/vision to a colleague or accountability partner. This stake-in-the-ground will serve as a commitment to taking your next step in creating it; even if you need to do some preliminary work like putting a time line together, or committing to research in order to make an informed step.

As always, make sure your declaration aligns with your mission and your values for maximum personal power in the process of making it happen!

ACTION

Declare what you want to do (put your stake in the ground!)

One thing you will do this week to signify that you have put your stake in the ground:

_____
_____
_____
_____
_____

Remember, if you find you don't like what you've staked out, you have the power to move it!

Inspired Action and Results

The Week in Action

Monday
Action Taken:

Hurdles Encountered:

The Plan to Move Forward Tomorrow:

Tuesday
Action Taken:

Hurdles Encountered:

The Plan to Move Forward Tomorrow:

Wednesday
Action Taken:

Hurdles Encountered:

The Plan to Move Forward Tomorrow:

Thursday
Action Taken:

Hurdles Encountered:

The Plan to Move Forward Tomorrow:

Friday
Action Taken:

Hurdles Encountered:

The Plan to Move Forward Tomorrow:

After stating your plan, gain support by identifying an accountability partner to share implementation updates weekly - both progress and hurdles.

The Slight Edge

Very small changes can have a huge impact over time. This, in essence, is what author Jeff Olson refers to in his book on success entitled *The Slight Edge*[4].

Frequently people think success comes through big breakthroughs or quantum leaps, yet a powerful success philosophy that is both doable and sustainable is The Slight Edge - taking a slight amount of action each day that moves you closer to your desired outcomes.

For instance, if you want to get in better physical shape, the slight edge works for you when you start exercising 20 minutes each day. Yet the slight edge can work against you as well. We don't achieve our goals when we take action that moves us away from them. The slight edge works against you if you decide to eat a second dessert regularly. Neither of these choices - daily walking or daily desserts, will have a big impact on you over the first few weeks, yet over time those slight edge choices will begin to show up in your waistline! This philosophy can be applied to reducing debt, saving for retirement, growing your business and

Inspired Action and Results

improving your relationships as well. Small, consistent choices over time add up to big results!

The author uses the following example to show the power of *The Slight Edge* philosophy. If you were to improve just .003 each day - that's only three-tenths of one percent, a very slight edge - and you kept that up for the next five years, here's what would happen:

- The first year you would improve 100 percent.
- The third year you would improve 400 percent.
- By the end of year five - simply by improving three-tenths of one percent per day - you will have magnified your value, your skills, and the results you accomplished 1600 percent!

ACTION

What "slight edge" action will you begin this week to move towards your desired future?

_____
_____
_____
_____
_____

Inspired Achievement

The Week in Action

Monday
Action Taken:

Hurdles Encountered:

The Plan to Move Forward Tomorrow:

Tuesday
Action Taken:

Hurdles Encountered:

The Plan to Move Forward Tomorrow:

Wednesday
Action Taken:

Hurdles Encountered:

The Plan to Move Forward Tomorrow:

Thursday
Action Taken:

Hurdles Encountered:

The Plan to Move Forward Tomorrow:

Friday
Action Taken:

Hurdles Encountered:

The Plan to Move Forward Tomorrow:

We are what we repeatedly do. Excellence, then, is not an act, but a habit - Aristotle

---

Inspired Action and Results

Aim Your Arrow at Your Target!

---◆---

THE CHALLENGE

The concept seems so simple. If you want to hit the target, point your arrow at the target! When aiming for a goal, it seems obvious to put your focus, energy and actions on the target you have chosen. And if your arrow is pointed in another direction, it is unlikely that the target will be achieved.

But how often have you found yourself aiming at something other than your desired goal or dream? Think about your goal. What actions move you in the direction that supports hitting your target? And what actions are aimed somewhere else – somewhere that could decrease your ability to hit your target?

Maybe it seems to hard, or maybe we are too fearful to really go after what we want - whatever the reason, the fact remains that in order to hit the target, you will need to aim at it. In order to achieve your goal, take actions to support reaching the target, and eliminate the actions that do not aim at your goal!

Inspired Achievement

This week I challenge you to define your target and clearly state what actions you are taking each day to move closer to your goal. Step by step, you will achieve it.

What is the target you wish to reach?

_____
_____
_____
_____

Action for this week that aims your arrow towards your target:

_____
_____
_____
_____

One action you will stop taking because it moves you away from your target:

_____
_____
_____
_____
_____

Inspired Action and Results

The Week in Action

Monday
Action Taken:

Hurdles Encountered:

The Plan to Move Forward Tomorrow:

Tuesday
Action Taken:

Hurdles Encountered:

The Plan to Move Forward Tomorrow:

Wednesday
Action Taken:

Hurdles Encountered:

The Plan to Move Forward Tomorrow:

Thursday
Action Taken:

Hurdles Encountered:

The Plan to Move Forward Tomorrow:

Friday
Action Taken:

Hurdles Encountered:

The Plan to Move Forward Tomorrow:

> The best archers invest time and energy practicing so that it becomes more likely to hit the bull's-eye!

The Strength of Your Arrow

---◆---

In the previous tip, we took a look at aiming your arrow at your target.

This week consider the qualities of your arrow.

What makes your arrow (your goal or intention) move powerfully in the direction you want it to go? A great aim on your part, a steady arm and lots of practice are all needed.

And then there is the arrow itself. Does your arrow have structural integrity? Is it sturdy, with no kinks, bends or missing feathers? When your thoughts, feelings, words and actions are all aligned with your target, this creates a powerful force - a sturdy arrow moving to achieve your desired target. This week take a look to see how your actions, your values and the words you use are all in alignment. This will help you move powerfully towards your desired target goal.

Inspired Action and Results

One thought that will help me move powerfully towards my goal:

_____
_____
_____
_____

One action I am taking this week that will also move me towards my goal:

_____
_____
_____
_____

This week take time each day to acknowledge your power to make it happen!

Feelings: Are you energized by, or compelled towards your target? Do you feel a lightness knowing that you will achieve it? If not, it may be time for a shift in your thinking, or a change of target.

Words: What are you saying to yourself and others about moving in the direction of your dreams? Are you affirming your desired goal? Or do you find yourself using words like "trying," "maybe," "if," etc.?

Actions: Each day take one specific action that moves you closer to your target. It may be as simple as visualizing the target, or asking for what you need to make it happen.

Inspired Achievement

The Week in Action

Monday
Action Taken:

Hurdles Encountered:

The Plan to Move Forward Tomorrow:

Tuesday
Action Taken:

Hurdles Encountered:

The Plan to Move Forward Tomorrow:

Wednesday
Action Taken:

Hurdles Encountered:

The Plan to Move Forward Tomorrow:

Thursday
Action Taken:

Hurdles Encountered:

The Plan to Move Forward Tomorrow:

Friday
Action Taken:

Hurdles Encountered:

The Plan to Move Forward Tomorrow:

Your brain listens to what you tell it! Identify the thoughts you tell yourself each day to promote your success.

Overcoming Obstacles to Achievement

What is your number one obstacle to achievement? I recently read an article by author Laura K. Bryant[5], and she says that the answer is usually related to lack of time or procrastination. But these reasons are really excuses that hide a deeper truth. They are the stories we tell ourselves when we're not willing to make something enough of a priority to invest the time and resources.

The number one obstacle to achievement is NOT making a true decision to achieve. The word decision is Latin in origin with de meaning "from" and caedere meaning "to cut." To decide literally means to commit to an outcome while cutting yourself off from any other possibility; there is no other option than to succeed.

Have you ever heard yourself say things such as, "I want to get more clients," or "I really need to get in better shape," or "I've been trying to read that book?" These are not decisions.

Rather they are things you might get done…when there's enough time…someday.

When researching people who consistently succeed, they do four things.

They:

1. Decide what they want

2. Take consistent, persistent action to get it

3. Review what works and what doesn't, and

4. Change what they're doing until they succeed

ACTION

Name one thing you want to achieve:

_____
_____
_____
_____

What commitment will you make to achieve it:

_____
_____
_____
_____

Inspired Action and Results

One thing you will do today to put this in motion:

_____
_____
_____
_____
_____

Inspired Achievement

The Week in Action

Monday
Action Taken:

Hurdles Encountered:

The Plan to Move Forward Tomorrow:

Tuesday
Action Taken:

Hurdles Encountered:

The Plan to Move Forward Tomorrow:

Wednesday
Action Taken:

Hurdles Encountered:

The Plan to Move Forward Tomorrow:

Thursday
Action Taken:

Hurdles Encountered:

The Plan to Move Forward Tomorrow:

Friday
Action Taken:

Hurdles Encountered:

The Plan to Move Forward Tomorrow:

Identify the support and resources you need to make your decision a reality. Invest in your decision to succeed!

Making SMART Goals SPICY!

By now you've heard about SMART Goals – Specific, Measurable, Achievable, Realistic and Time Limited. Creating goals in this manner will help you clarify if you are achieving them.

However, what is it that makes you WANT to achieve your goals? Or, as I like to ask:

What makes your goal SPICY?

S – Synergistic goals serve your needs as well as the needs of others involved. Your values are in alignment and all involved are energized by the thought of achieving the goal.

P – Your goal *packs a punch!* It has *pizzazz* and propels you towards it!

I – It is Irresistible! Need I say more? You are drawn to it like a moth to a flame!

C – Compelling – you see NO reason NOT to complete your goal – it makes total sense and is something you want to attain!

Y – Your desired future is reflected in achieving this goal. It's where you REALLY want to go!

Inspired Achievement

The Invitation: This week I want to invite you to look at your goals and see how attractive they are to you. Then consider what would make your goals SPICY:

1. Make sure it's big enough! Sometimes we don't move towards the goal because it isn't big enough for us to really get energized by it.
2. Ask, "Is it in alignment with my values?" If not, I will not be able to put my full energy into it.
3. Share the goals with your support team and create accountability. Does everyone involved see how it relates to them and their needs?

ACTION

The Goal:

_____
_____
_____
_____

How I will make it "Spicy!"

_____
_____
_____
_____

Inspired Action and Results

The Week in Action

Monday

Action Taken:

Hurdles Encountered:

The Plan to Move Forward Tomorrow:

Tuesday

Action Taken:

Hurdles Encountered:

The Plan to Move Forward Tomorrow:

Wednesday

Action Taken:

Hurdles Encountered:

The Plan to Move Forward Tomorrow:

Thursday

Action Taken:

Hurdles Encountered:

The Plan to Move Forward Tomorrow:

Friday

Action Taken:

Hurdles Encountered:

The Plan to Move Forward Tomorrow:

Life is a daring adventure, or nothing! -Helen Keller

"*Being*" To Get Results

───────◆───────

"How does one become a butterfly?" she asked pensively. "You must want to fly so much that you are willing to give up being a caterpillar." — Trina Paulus

What is it that you long to create for your life? It may be in your career, or it may have to do with getting healthier, wealthier, or attracting dynamic people into your life. All of these things are possible for you!

In his book *Good to Great*[6], author Jim Collins explains why some companies never make the leap to move from good to great. It's sounds so simple, yet it's profound. They are satisfied being good. That's it. The satisfaction of being "good enough" becomes the enemy of becoming great.

The caveat is this: Are you willing to give up the way things are for you today to create something different for your tomorrow? It's that simple, yet that challenging at the same time.

Inspired Action and Results

What is "that something" you want to create for your life?
_____
_____
_____
_____
_____

What would need to "be" different in order to achieve that?
_____
_____
_____
_____
_____

What might you do today to put that into motion?
_____
_____
_____
_____
_____

THE INVITATION

Show up differently tomorrow and see what you create!

The Week in Action

Monday

Action Taken:

Hurdles Encountered:

The Plan to Move Forward Tomorrow:

Tuesday

Action Taken:

Hurdles Encountered:

The Plan to Move Forward Tomorrow:

Wednesday

Action Taken:

Hurdles Encountered:

The Plan to Move Forward Tomorrow:

Thursday

Action Taken:

Hurdles Encountered:

The Plan to Move Forward Tomorrow:

Friday

Action Taken:

Hurdles Encountered:

The Plan to Move Forward Tomorrow:

If you find that you are not ready to alter your choices or behavior to get better results, write down what you need to begin preparing for that change and clarify if this is something you truly desire for yourself and your life at this time. What would make the time right for you to begin?

Inspired Action and Results

Accountability as a Power Tool

♦

When you hear the word *accountability* what comes up for you? Say it out loud a couple of times and take notice. Does the term inspire thoughts of determination and increased success?

Today I invite you to see accountability as a power tool to increase your success!

When you have a goal to reach, creating accountability is one sure way to strengthen your achievement. As a coach, I have my own "accountability partner." We meet every Monday morning for 20 minutes to state our goals and specific actions for the week. Then we send each other a brief text to share successes and setbacks, while providing encouragement along the way. It has been a dynamic and enjoyable partnership in reaching new goals.

Below are 4 steps to create your own Accountability Power Tool.

1. Choose someone who will challenge and support you in reaching your goals. Be sure this person is someone

you are willing to get to know well. You are sharing your goals and dreams with them, and they with you.

2. Schedule a brief weekly meeting by phone, text or email, and use the time specifically for stating your goals and actions. (Refrain from using this time for a social discussion. Feel free to set another time for that.)

3. Each week take 10 minutes (or less) to state a big goal you are working on, and specific action you will take during that week to move towards your goal. Let the other person challenge you to stretch your actions if you like. You can accept or decline the stretch!

4. At the next call, review successes and setbacks, and state your actions for the following week.

QUESTIONS TO MOVE YOU FORWARD:

I want an accountability partner with this goal:

_____
_____
_____
_____
_____

The person I will ask to be my accountability partner:

_____
_____
_____
_____

Inspired Action and Results

THE WEEK IN ACTION

MONDAY
Action Taken:

Hurdles Encountered:

The Plan to Move Forward Tomorrow:

TUESDAY
Action Taken:

Hurdles Encountered:

The Plan to Move Forward Tomorrow:

WEDNESDAY
Action Taken:

Hurdles Encountered:

The Plan to Move Forward Tomorrow:

THURSDAY
Action Taken:

Hurdles Encountered:

The Plan to Move Forward Tomorrow:

FRIDAY
Action Taken:

Hurdles Encountered:

The Plan to Move Forward Tomorrow:

You do not rise to the level of your goals; you fall to the level of your systems. -James Clear, author of **Atomic Habits**

One Thing

Take a moment, close your eyes and think of one thing that, if you would change it, shift it, add it or subtract it, would make a significant difference in your success.

What is that one thing?

_____
_____
_____
_____

Are you ready to move on your journey by making this change?

What keeps you from moving on it?

_____
_____
_____
_____

Inspired Action and Results

What are you willing to do this week to handle that one thing that keeps you from moving towards it?

_____
_____
_____
_____
_____

This is your life! Take advantage of the opportunities to make your "one thing" a reality beginning today.

Inspired Achievement

The Week in Action

Monday
Action Taken:

Hurdles Encountered:

The Plan to Move Forward Tomorrow:

Tuesday
Action Taken:

Hurdles Encountered:

The Plan to Move Forward Tomorrow:

Wednesday
Action Taken:

Hurdles Encountered:

The Plan to Move Forward Tomorrow:

Thursday
Action Taken:

Hurdles Encountered:

The Plan to Move Forward Tomorrow:

Friday
Action Taken:

Hurdles Encountered:

The Plan to Move Forward Tomorrow:

This week, take action to impact that one thing, and like a pebble thrown into the water, there will be a ripple-effect in your life.

Inspired Action and Results

The art of communication is the language of leadership.

James Humes

Lean In to Communication and Leadership

------♦------

Communicating thoughts, feelings, and your business message is paramount in attracting and retaining friends, colleagues and clients in our lives.

Understanding how to respond, how to listen, and even how to be silent, are all skills that make it possible to successfully navigate relationships even under the most challenging circumstances.

A recent article at HRtechnologist.com stated that 57% of employees report not being given clear directions at work, and 69% of the supervisors were not comfortable giving directions to their team, making it clear that we need to strengthen our workplace communication[7].

Communication:

- Decreases confusion
- Increases clarity
- Provides purpose
- Builds a positive working relationship
- Creates accountability that leads to greater success

As with most skills, it takes time and practice to hone them. Since strengthening communication is a "practice," give yourself grace and know that it won't be perfect! Author Ken Blanchard wrote a book called, *The One Minute Apology*[8]. It is important to know the skill of apologizing because communication can easily be misunderstood, and a genuine apology can be like water to a parched soul when our words or actions have caused confusion or pain.

Tips to improve communication:

- Tell people what they are doing well regularly
- Give specific and descriptive feedback
- Schedule regular check-in time for questions and ensure all understand assignments
- Engage the team with team building activities
- View feedback as a conversational development opportunity

A Quick Tip for Improving Relationships

♦

In the emerging field of positive psychology, Dr. Shelly Gable has found that using an *active, constructive response* to positive news helps strengthen relationships.[9]

An *active, constructive, response* conveys enthusiasm, support and interest in response to news that someone is sharing with you. For example, your partner shares that they got a promotion at work. The *active, constructive response* would look something like this: "That's great, you've earned it. I'm so proud of you!" Followed by questions of interest like: "When do you start? How are you feeling about the change?" etc.

Dr. Gable also identified three other responses that are NOT helpful in creating a better relationship. They include:

1. The passive, constructive response – This would include a brief, affirmative statement like, "Great job," but then quickly shift the conversation on to something else without asking follow up questions.

Inspired Action and Results

2. The active, destructive response (or "finding a cloud in a silver lining") – This would include saying something like, "Wow, does that mean you'll be home later, or have to put in more hours?"

3. The passive, destructive response – This response would basically ignore the positive news and quickly turn the focus back to the person who was responding: i.e. "Wow, wait until I tell you what happened to me today," which is very self-focused, or "What's for dinner?" - which just ignores the event all together.

So as you work to strengthen your relationship with your family, your colleagues and your clients, practice the active, constructive response this week. The *Active, Constructive Response* (with an example):

1. An affirming response. "That's great, you've earned it and I am so proud of you!

2. Followed by questions of interest. What are you most excited about with your new job?

ACTION

One way I will practice the *active constructive response* this week:

_____
_____
_____
_____
_____

The Week in Action

Monday
Action Taken:

Hurdles Encountered:

The Plan to Move Forward Tomorrow:

Tuesday
Action Taken:

Hurdles Encountered:

The Plan to Move Forward Tomorrow:

Wednesday
Action Taken:

Hurdles Encountered:

The Plan to Move Forward Tomorrow:

Thursday
Action Taken:

Hurdles Encountered:

The Plan to Move Forward Tomorrow:

Friday
Action Taken:

Hurdles Encountered:

The Plan to Move Forward Tomorrow:

Be sure to listen to the answer, and ask another follow-up question or reflect back something you heard.

Inspired Action and Results

Courageous Conversations

---◆---

A courageous conversation usually needs to occur when a situation is tugging at you, causing you to expend emotional energy and thought. Generally, the conversation needs to happen in order for you to resolve something and move forward in a meaningful way. It may include things like speaking to a team member who isn't meeting goals, asking a client for a referral, or letting a friend know that you can't keep listening to their daily complaints.

Many times we don't dive into the important conversations in life because it seems intimidating or overwhelming. Maybe it's that we don't feel like we are in the right frame of mind, or we doubt our words and attitude would adequately express what needs to be said. Yet like building a muscle, courageous conversations take practice over time to get good at them.

This week take time to experiment with a courageous conversation.

Here are a few tips to get started:

1. Identify with whom you need to have the conversation.
2. Decide what you want out of the conversation – maybe you just want to be heard, or it could be for the purpose of getting a specific action.
3. If needed, write down what you will say and practice it in the mirror or with a trusted friend. I've actually put my key points on note cards when I want to be sure to cover the important points.
4. Ask for a few minutes (or schedule a meeting) to have the conversation. Be sure this person has time to talk before starting the conversation.
5. Take responsibility for your feelings rather than blaming or accusing someone else. Try this formula "Bob, yesterday I felt ____(upset) when you said that _____(my team wasn't getting the results we had agreed on) because (we have met our quarterly goals.)
6. Don't make it personal and don't take it personally! It's all a learning, growing experience.

This week redefine winning with a courageous conversation.

The win: Both people have the opportunity to express their viewpoint and feel heard in the process. Schedule a follow-up time to consider options for resolution if needed. If this seems too risky, contact me for options to move forward with confidence.

Inspired Action and Results

One person I want to have the courageous conversation with and what my next step is to make that happen:

_____
_____
_____
_____
_____

THE WEEK IN ACTION

MONDAY
Action Taken:

Hurdles Encountered:

The Plan to Move Forward Tomorrow:

TUESDAY
Action Taken:

Hurdles Encountered:

The Plan to Move Forward Tomorrow:

WEDNESDAY
Action Taken:

Hurdles Encountered:

The Plan to Move Forward Tomorrow:

THURSDAY
Action Taken:

Hurdles Encountered:

The Plan to Move Forward Tomorrow:

FRIDAY
Action Taken:

Hurdles Encountered:

The Plan to Move Forward Tomorrow:

Courage is what it takes to stand up and talk; courage is also what it takes to sit down and listen. -Winston Churchill

Inspired Action and Results

Positive Moments of Truth

Brief affirming actions, or instant connections with others are called "positive moments of truth."[10]

These moments of truth occur when you have contact with others that leads them to form a positive impression about you based on that one contact. These moments of truth usually take no longer than 20 seconds, but have a LASTING IMPRESSION on others' perception of you and the organization you represent.

Several examples of positive moments of truth:

- Offering to make an additional call to get an answer to a client's question
- Looking a client in the eyes
- Getting the person what they need right in that moment
- Calling someone back immediately
- Answering the phone with a smile (they can hear it in your voice!)

Talk with your colleagues about how you are each creating these positive moments, and ensure they are happening regularly.

ACTION

One positive moment of truth you will increase this week:

_____
_____
_____
_____
_____

Inspired Action and Results

The Week in Action

Monday
Action Taken:

Hurdles Encountered:

The Plan to Move Forward Tomorrow:

Tuesday
Action Taken:

Hurdles Encountered:

The Plan to Move Forward Tomorrow:

Wednesday
Action Taken:

Hurdles Encountered:

The Plan to Move Forward Tomorrow:

Thursday
Action Taken:

Hurdles Encountered:

The Plan to Move Forward Tomorrow:

Friday
Action Taken:

Hurdles Encountered:

The Plan to Move Forward Tomorrow:

Create positive moments for your team members and your family, as well as your clients! It will strengthen your connection to each person.

The Law of Recency: What have you done for me LATELY?

———◆———

In the early 1900's psychologist Edward Thorndike coined several "Laws of Learning." His "Law of Recency"[11] states that things you have learned or encountered most recently are best remembered (and can interfere with old learning.)

In business and in life this translates in a couple of significant ways:

1. Even if you had a difficult transaction previously (old learning), you can do something now that will strengthen the relationship, and there is a chance that your most recent interaction with the customer will be remembered more vividly than the previous, problem interaction.

2. If you have a good relationship with your clients, yet haven't done anything recently that would remind them of your good will, (such as sending a note, a phone call, etc.) NOT taking positive, proaction can

Inspired Action and Results

erode your relationship. (This works for personal relationships as well.)

This week I invite you to continue to connect with your clients (and potential clients) through personal contact, follow up, special events, etc. Let them know you are there and do something that puts you in the forefront of their thinking!

ACTION

One way I will use the "Law of Recency" this week:

_____
_____
_____
_____
_____

THE WEEK IN ACTION

MONDAY

Action Taken:

Hurdles Encountered:

The Plan to Move Forward Tomorrow:

TUESDAY

Action Taken:

Hurdles Encountered:

The Plan to Move Forward Tomorrow:

WEDNESDAY

Action Taken:

Hurdles Encountered:

The Plan to Move Forward Tomorrow:

THURSDAY

Action Taken:

Hurdles Encountered:

The Plan to Move Forward Tomorrow:

FRIDAY

Action Taken:

Hurdles Encountered:

The Plan to Move Forward Tomorrow:

Take action to create a positive experience with your team, your family and your clients this week.

The Only Way to Lead

Recently, I met a new neighbor, a young military man and his two-year-old son who was not quite talking yet, but was at that phase where he was babbling a-mile-a-minute, and seemed to know exactly what he was saying, just nothing that I could understand.

We were all returning from the neighborhood mail boxes, chatting and walking down the middle of our quiet street. The vocal toddler walked in the street with us, while his dad asked him several times to move over to the side walk. I couldn't help but share my own learning with the young father. "You can tell them what you want all day long, but they will ultimately do what they see you doing." As we both moved over to walk on the sidewalk with a chuckle, the toddler followed right behind us, chattering all the way back to the house, never realizing how he had become the teacher, helping his father learn a big lesson that day!

ACTION

One way I will practice leading-by-example this week:

_____
_____
_____
_____

Inspired Action and Results

The Week in Action

Monday
Action Taken:

Hurdles Encountered:

The Plan to Move Forward Tomorrow:

Tuesday
Action Taken:

Hurdles Encountered:

The Plan to Move Forward Tomorrow:

Wednesday
Action Taken:

Hurdles Encountered:

The Plan to Move Forward Tomorrow:

Thursday
Action Taken:

Hurdles Encountered:

The Plan to Move Forward Tomorrow:

Friday
Action Taken:

Hurdles Encountered:

The Plan to Move Forward Tomorrow:

Example is not the main thing in influencing others – it is the only thing. – Albert Schweitzer

Try Not!

Today I would like to invite you to stop trying to get the results you want. Yes, I really did say "stop trying!" Today is the day to stop trying…and instead put into motion the actions that will get you there!

Words are incredibly powerful. When you say you are "trying to lose weight" or "trying to start a new process at work" it sounds as though there is a strong chance that you won't make it. This language takes away from the power of your resolve. Instead of "trying", use statements like "I am losing weight starting today," or "We are implementing a new process that will be fully operational by the end of August." Your mind responds to the messages that you speak. Make your statements powerful and see how "not trying" will help you achieve the results you really want!

Inspired Action and Results

ACTION

One thing you have been "trying" to accomplish:

_____
_____
_____
_____

Your revised statement of resolve to do it:

_____
_____
_____
_____

Action you are taking this week to move you in the direction of your goal:

_____
_____
_____
_____

Go get 'um!

Lean In to Communication and Leadership

The Week in Action

Monday
Action Taken:

Hurdles Encountered:

The Plan to Move Forward Tomorrow:

Tuesday
Action Taken:

Hurdles Encountered:

The Plan to Move Forward Tomorrow:

Wednesday
Action Taken:

Hurdles Encountered:

The Plan to Move Forward Tomorrow:

Thursday
Action Taken:

Hurdles Encountered:

The Plan to Move Forward Tomorrow:

Friday
Action Taken:

Hurdles Encountered:

The Plan to Move Forward Tomorrow:

> Try not! Do or do not. There is no try. –
> Yoda (Star Wars Jedi Master)

Fit not Fault

We've all heard of a "no fault" automobile accident, and now I'd like to invite you to apply this principle of "no fault" to work-related situations that aren't working well.

Frequently when we want to find fault, it is done to help assuage personal guilt over needing to change the status of the relationship. It may be the need to let a client go, or to end a collegial relationship that is no longer working.

I was once asked to "counsel" someone out of applying for a job position. At first this idea was offensive to me. Yet when I saw that the job required skills and resources that this person did not have, it actually made sense to talk with this person and help them identify their true strengths and see how the job being considered would not use the strengths, and would also require other skills that were not a part of this person's repertoire, eventually leading to a sense of frustration and failure rather than future career success.

Finding a "good fit" in the people you work with is essential for success for both of you! If you are working with someone who isn't a good fit, instead of needing to find fault to justify new action, how about looking at it from a "fit" perspective? Is this person the best fit for what you are creating at this time? Maybe they were a great fit when the company was smaller, but as the circumstances changed, what they are bringing to your practice in terms of energy and resources may no longer serve either of you well. Having an honest conversation with a trusted friend or colleague about what skills are really needed to have success in the role may help you come to a decision that better serves all involved. You might even consider a rewrite of the job description to more specifically outline what skills are needed for future hires.

Now apply this!

ACTION

A situation where I am currently "finding fault":

_____
_____
_____
_____

How I will turn this situation into an issue of "fit not fault:"

_____
_____
_____
_____

Inspired Action and Results

The Week in Action

Monday
Action Taken:

Hurdles Encountered:

The Plan to Move Forward Tomorrow:

Tuesday
Action Taken:

Hurdles Encountered:

The Plan to Move Forward Tomorrow:

Wednesday
Action Taken:

Hurdles Encountered:

The Plan to Move Forward Tomorrow:

Thursday
Action Taken:

Hurdles Encountered:

The Plan to Move Forward Tomorrow:

Friday
Action Taken:

Hurdles Encountered:

The Plan to Move Forward Tomorrow:

> Infuse your courageous conversation about "fit"
> with genuine care and support.

The Extra Degree

There is a short book out called *The Extra Degree*.[12] It starts something like this:

"At 211 degrees, water is hot. At 212 degrees, it boils. And boiling water can create the steam needed to power a locomotive. One extra degree makes all the difference."

Today I want to challenge you to "turn it up" one degree.

- Where in your career or your life would one degree give you an edge that you currently desire?
- Are you ready to turn it up?

Do what it takes to turn it up and see the difference in the results you achieve!

Inspired Action and Results

ACTION

The area of my life where I want to turn it up:

_____
_____
_____
_____
_____

What it will take to turn it up:

_____
_____
_____
_____
_____

How I will begin today:

_____
_____
_____
_____
_____

THE WEEK IN ACTION

MONDAY
Action Taken:

Hurdles Encountered:

The Plan to Move Forward Tomorrow:

TUESDAY
Action Taken:

Hurdles Encountered:

The Plan to Move Forward Tomorrow:

WEDNESDAY
Action Taken:

Hurdles Encountered:

The Plan to Move Forward Tomorrow:

THURSDAY
Action Taken:

Hurdles Encountered:

The Plan to Move Forward Tomorrow:

FRIDAY
Action Taken:

Hurdles Encountered:

The Plan to Move Forward Tomorrow:

Turn it up this week. Take an extra degree of action to create your 212 degree life!

Inspired Action and Results

Taking Flight

―――――♦―――――

It was an inspiring visit to Kitty Hawk, North Carolina where just a little over 100 years ago the Wright brothers were the first to successfully fly an air plane.[13] I noticed a few points that seemed foundational in making their dream take flight and I'd like to share them with you.

1. It started with a dream - The Wright brothers were bicycle repair guys who had a dream of taking flight.

2. They were passionate about making it happen - They actually packed up and moved to Kitty Hawk where they could focus on their goal, leaving everything else behind for a time.

3. They had each other for support and accountability - Having a brother there who believed in the project was like putting wind beneath each other's wings. When they were frustrated, they consoled and challenged each other to keep moving.

4. Even when it seemed impossible, they kept trying - In 1901 Orville Wright said it would be a thousand years before man took flight. Two years later, in 1903, they successfully took flight - four times in one day, going a bit further each time they launched.

5. They had no idea how greatly their achievement would impact us today - They had a dream, and others continue to build on their dream, so that it changes the way we live and work and will continue to make a profound impact on humankind.

So today, I invite you to:

1. Acknowledge your dream.
2. Be passionate about making it happen.
3. Have people in your life who believe in your success and provide accountability.
4. Even when it seems impossible, keep believing in your dream.
5. Know that what you achieve today may have a future impact completely unknown to you.

What is the dream that you wish to move forward?

_____

_____

This week, how will you commit to making it happen?

_____

_____

Inspired Action and Results

The Week in Action

Monday

Action Taken:

Hurdles Encountered:

The Plan to Move Forward Tomorrow:

Tuesday

Action Taken:

Hurdles Encountered:

The Plan to Move Forward Tomorrow:

Wednesday

Action Taken:

Hurdles Encountered:

The Plan to Move Forward Tomorrow:

Thursday

Action Taken:

Hurdles Encountered:

The Plan to Move Forward Tomorrow:

Friday

Action Taken:

Hurdles Encountered:

The Plan to Move Forward Tomorrow:

Begin the action that will make your dream take flight!

And the day came when the risk to remain tight in a bud was more painful than the risk it took to bloom.

Anais Nin

AUTHENTIC YOU

---◆---

We each bring unique gifts to the world. As we move through life, our unique gifts are often hidden due to some anxiety or fear about being vulnerable and sharing who we are with others. What will happen if we fully express who we are and what we want in life? Until we are willing to risk sharing our hearts and our dreams, we never fully connect with others. Authenticity, the ability to be genuine, to show vulnerability and care, seems too great a risk and too large a task for many. So we hide, sometimes by staying small and in our comfort zones, other times behind the pursuit of nice things and nice cars, hoping people will see us in the context of our belongings, rather than having to see one another heart-to-heart. The good news is that being authentically you opens you up to the greatest adventure of all...your authentic life.

In her book entitled *A Return to Love*,[14] Mariannne Williamson reminds us that there is a deep truth and a calling in regards to our unique gifts. She writes:

Our deepest fear is not that we are inadequate.

Our deepest fear is that we are powerful beyond measure.

It is our light, not our darkness

That most frightens us.

We ask ourselves

Who am I to be brilliant, gorgeous, talented, fabulous?

Actually, who are you not to be?

You are a child of God.

Your playing small

Does not serve the world.

There's nothing enlightened about shrinking

So that other people won't feel insecure around you.

We are all meant to shine,

As children do.

We were born to make manifest

The glory of God that is within us.

It's not just in some of us;

It's in everyone.

And as we let our own light shine,

We unconsciously give other people permission to do the same.

As we're liberated from our own fear,

Our presence automatically liberates others.

Inspired Action and Results

As we play big and stretch fully into the amazing beings we were designed to become, we give others permission, encouragement, and an example of how to manifest, liberating each other from a life of self-limitation.

An Infusion of Joy

Recently, while spending a few days in California, I was introduced to drinking water infused with all kinds of fruits, flowers, and other creative spices. This led me to think about our lives, and what we infuse into them that brings us joy, including people, places and particular items and traditions that spark something special in us.

For this week, I invite you to infuse your activities, duties, and adventures with JOY! Infusing your experiences with joy is like creating your own designer experience.

What is it that brings you joy? Is it…

- Listening to great music
- Socializing with friends
- Baking delicious treats
- Doing a special project for someone in need
- Or maybe it's taking time to sit down and read a few pages of a great book in the midst of it all.

Inspired Action and Results

Whatever it is that brings you joy, infuse it into your daily activities. Plan for it, do it, experience it!

One thing that brings me joy:

_____
_____
_____
_____

One way I will infuse it into my week:

_____
_____
_____
_____

Create the joy you wish to experience in the world!

The Week in Action

Monday
Action Taken:

Hurdles Encountered:

The Plan to Move Forward Tomorrow:

Tuesday
Action Taken:

Hurdles Encountered:

The Plan to Move Forward Tomorrow:

Wednesday
Action Taken:

Hurdles Encountered:

The Plan to Move Forward Tomorrow:

Thursday
Action Taken:

Hurdles Encountered:

The Plan to Move Forward Tomorrow:

Friday
Action Taken:

Hurdles Encountered:

The Plan to Move Forward Tomorrow:

Intentionally infuse joy and inspiration into your daily life.

Inspired Action and Results

Care for Your Heart!

◆

We've all heard the public service announcements about stress and how it can be harmful to the heart. In fact, the CDC reports that cardiovascular issues rank as the top cause of death in the United States (www.CDC. gov).[15]

The good news is that we can take action to care for our hearts. We have each been given one spectacular heart, and it has a round-the-clock job beating for us! Take time to care for the heart that works so faithfully for you!

Here are some simple tips to care for your heart:

Stay positive – Laughter has been found to lower levels of stress hormones, reduce inflammation and increase "good" HDL cholesterol.

Meditate –Take a few minutes daily to focus on your state-of-being. Breathe in deeply and exhale slowly. Deep breathing has been shown to relax the mind and body, reducing heart disease risk factors.

Exercise – Every time you are physically active, your body releases mood-boosting chemicals! Try something you enjoy.

Even standing up and walking up and down the stairs or around the hallways will get you moving, and will give you an opportunity to say hello to others as you move - ask a friend to join you, or call a friend while you're on the move.

Unplug – Take time each day, even if it's just a few minutes, to unplug from all the stress! You decide what that looks like for you.

Take the edge off your stress – Simple things, like listening to music or spending time with your favorite hobby can give you a much-needed break from the stressors of life.

The Invitation: How will you be kind to your heart this week?

_____
_____
_____
_____
_____

Inspired Action and Results

The Week in Action

Monday

Action Taken:

Hurdles Encountered:

The Plan to Move Forward Tomorrow:

Tuesday

Action Taken:

Hurdles Encountered:

The Plan to Move Forward Tomorrow:

Wednesday

Action Taken:

Hurdles Encountered:

The Plan to Move Forward Tomorrow:

Thursday

Action Taken:

Hurdles Encountered:

The Plan to Move Forward Tomorrow:

Friday

Action Taken:

Hurdles Encountered:

The Plan to Move Forward Tomorrow:

Create daily action that incorporates healthy thoughts, nutrition and exercise as part of your best life!

The Gift of the Life You Desire

❖

What would it take for you to receive the gift of living the life you desire? What change would make a big difference in your life? It could be advancing your career, losing extra pounds, or getting help to deal with a challenging situation, just to name a few.

You know your deepest desires for a great life, and I invite you to make it happen.

ACTION

One thing that would help me to live the life I desire:

_____
_____
_____
_____

Inspired Action and Results

One way I will commit to making it happen for myself:

_____
_____
_____
_____

This is your life. Take charge and make it what you want it to be!

The Week in Action

Monday
Action Taken:

Hurdles Encountered:

The Plan to Move Forward Tomorrow:

Tuesday
Action Taken:

Hurdles Encountered:

The Plan to Move Forward Tomorrow:

Wednesday
Action Taken:

Hurdles Encountered:

The Plan to Move Forward Tomorrow:

Thursday
Action Taken:

Hurdles Encountered:

The Plan to Move Forward Tomorrow:

Friday
Action Taken:

Hurdles Encountered:

The Plan to Move Forward Tomorrow:

Create a new mindset! View everything that happens this week as information illuminating your path to the life you really want. Be in gratitude for it all.

Inspired Action and Results

Small Kindnesses

I recently attended a colleague's memorial service, where many recounted the small kindnesses that she had extended to staff, clients, and the community she served in her work as a receptionist.

It caused me to ponder… Is there really such a thing as small kindnesses? A cup of water (often free) is a BIG gift to a person who is thirsty. A smile or a word of encouragement to a person who is grieving can restore hope.

Reaching out to another human being and touching the heart is an act of kindness. And the beautiful thing about small is that small tends to be doable. So if small really exists in the world of kindness, maybe, just maybe, small is better.

May we all be inspired to live this legacy by extending small kindnesses each day!

THE INVITATION

Commit to an act of small kindness each day this week!

The Week in Action

Monday
Action Taken:

Hurdles Encountered:

The Plan to Move Forward Tomorrow:

Tuesday
Action Taken:

Hurdles Encountered:

The Plan to Move Forward Tomorrow:

Wednesday
Action Taken:

Hurdles Encountered:

The Plan to Move Forward Tomorrow:

Thursday
Action Taken:

Hurdles Encountered:

The Plan to Move Forward Tomorrow:

Friday
Action Taken:

Hurdles Encountered:

The Plan to Move Forward Tomorrow:

> Practice small kindnesses each day and notice how it impacts your mood. The Stretch Invitation: Invite colleagues to join you. Debrief to discuss the impact small kindnesses had on you and your world.

Inspired Action and Results

Surfing the Waves of Change

♦

Each day we find ourselves dealing with stress, worry and uncertainties both at home and at work. The effects of stress are linked to illness, dissatisfaction, and lower productivity.

How do you cope? Or even better, how do you ride the waves of stress and uncertainty?

I recommend a surf board. Now, this may not include going out to purchase an actual board - instead how about creating a visual that helps you to see the daily waves of stress as something that you are equipped to navigate with the skills and the resources you have – your surf board!

Our perspective on a situation tends to create our reality, so by visualizing yourself as a skilled surfer of life, with the tools necessary to manage the waves of uncertainty, you experience a greater sense of mastery, knowing that whatever comes your way, it is just another wave to be surfed. And if a wave knocks you down, use your board to float until you are ready to surf another wave! (Maybe even take a couple of surfing lessons to gain a new level of mastery!)

Authentic You

ACTION

One wave (stress or challenge) in my life I would like to start surfing:

_____
_____
_____
_____
_____

How I can view the situation differently that will have me surfing the wave:

_____
_____
_____
_____
_____

Something I will learn, or practice, to skillfully ride the wave:

_____
_____
_____
_____
_____

Inspired Action and Results

The Week in Action

Monday
Action Taken:

Hurdles Encountered:

The Plan to Move Forward Tomorrow:

Tuesday
Action Taken:

Hurdles Encountered:

The Plan to Move Forward Tomorrow:

Wednesday
Action Taken:

Hurdles Encountered:

The Plan to Move Forward Tomorrow:

Thursday
Action Taken:

Hurdles Encountered:

The Plan to Move Forward Tomorrow:

Friday
Action Taken:

Hurdles Encountered:

The Plan to Move Forward Tomorrow:

Acknowledge your personal strengths and the support team that ensures you are successfully surfing the challenging waves this week!

A New Day and a True You!

What is inspiring you to move forward powerfully today?

Assess yourself with this quick checklist!

- ☐ I know what I want to achieve/attain/accomplish.
- ☐ I have a plan for achieving it.
- ☐ I have access to the resources I need.
- ☐ All involved are fully engaged in the plan.
- ☐ I have built in the accountability I need to be successful.
- ☐ I know it will be worth my time.
- ☐ I am energized to do this!

Inspired Action and Results

When I look back on this year, what I want to be able to say is:

_____
_____
_____
_____

Create your desired future!

The Week in Action

Monday
Action Taken:

Hurdles Encountered:

The Plan to Move Forward Tomorrow:

Tuesday
Action Taken:

Hurdles Encountered:

The Plan to Move Forward Tomorrow:

Wednesday
Action Taken:

Hurdles Encountered:

The Plan to Move Forward Tomorrow:

Thursday
Action Taken:

Hurdles Encountered:

The Plan to Move Forward Tomorrow:

Friday
Action Taken:

Hurdles Encountered:

The Plan to Move Forward Tomorrow:

Many people hire a personal trainer or coach to achieve wellness goals. It's the same for your professional goals. Invest in the support system needed to achieve your success!

Inspired Action and Results

Living Your strengths

"What you do best is probably so easy you underestimate its value." Fred Smith, author of *You and your network; getting the most out of your life.*

What do you believe about yourself that makes it easy for you to succeed? (For example – I am a quick learner; Making money is easy for me; I enjoy organizing everything.)

Do you have the opportunity to use those strengths frequently in your career? Being in an environment that supports the use of your strengths increases your success.

We each bring unique strengths to the table:

1. Become aware of your strengths – Jot down your top 5 strengths. How are you using them in your work?

2. Help others see your strengths – Maybe they seem them, maybe they don't. Have a conversation with your team to let them know your natural strengths. Ask about their strengths as well.

3. Make, take and find opportunities that put your strengths to use –

    - ASK for what you want!

    - VOLUNTEER to be involved in something that would bring you joy.

    - STEP UP and request to be on a board or project that utilizes your strengths.

    - CREATE your own unique business attractor that utilizes your strengths while reflecting the mission of the company.

ACTION

Gain assistance in clarifying your strengths:

1. Ask 5 people who know you to name three strong points about you. Jot them down. Listen and thank them. No debates here.

_____
_____
_____

2. Read **Now Discover Your Strengths**[16] by Marcus Buckingham and Donald O. Clifton. The book comes with a code to take a strengths finder assessment on line and generates a report of your strengths.

_____
_____
_____

Inspired Action and Results

The Week in Action

Monday
Action Taken:

Hurdles Encountered:

The Plan to Move Forward Tomorrow:

Tuesday
Action Taken:

Hurdles Encountered:

The Plan to Move Forward Tomorrow:

Wednesday
Action Taken:

Hurdles Encountered:

The Plan to Move Forward Tomorrow:

Thursday
Action Taken:

Hurdles Encountered:

The Plan to Move Forward Tomorrow:

Friday
Action Taken:

Hurdles Encountered:

The Plan to Move Forward Tomorrow:

Being you is easy! Use your strengths to increase connection and experience greater ease in both your life and your career.

Being Who You Are

---◆---

While I've heard others talk about the struggle to "find themselves," another profound question has always been, "How can I be who I am?"

Being who I am. Sounds so simple.

- Is it easy being you?
- Do you find it effortless to be your authentic self?
- Fearless in asking for what you need?
- Is being true to your "Self" valued?

Ever find yourself saying something to please others, rather than stating your truth? The great Dr. Seuss said it so eloquently. "Be who you are and say what you feel, 'cause people who mind don't matter, and people who matter don't mind."

This week I challenge you to live in alignment with your authentic "Self." One way I will align with my authentic self this week is:

Inspired Action and Results

TO PONDER

What looks different in your life when aligned with your true Self?

_____
_____
_____
_____
_____

The Week in Action

Monday
Action Taken:

Hurdles Encountered:

The Plan to Move Forward Tomorrow:

Tuesday
Action Taken:

Hurdles Encountered:

The Plan to Move Forward Tomorrow:

Wednesday
Action Taken:

Hurdles Encountered:

The Plan to Move Forward Tomorrow:

Thursday
Action Taken:

Hurdles Encountered:

The Plan to Move Forward Tomorrow:

Friday
Action Taken:

Hurdles Encountered:

The Plan to Move Forward Tomorrow:

Practice one new way to be authentically you this week!

Get Your Needs Met

We all know that we need things like air, water, food and shelter. These are some of our physical needs. But what about personal needs? These are the things we require in order to be our best selves, yet frequently we find that we are not able to get "enough" of them.

For example, I worked with a client who thrives in an environment with lots of social interaction, community outreach, and positive energy. Yet after moving across the country, this person began spending a lot of time alone and was not getting those needs met. Once the needs were identified, we brainstormed a list of ways to meet them. This person decided to join a community organization that supports many social causes, and is now flourishing there.

When a person is getting their needs fully met:

- They have room and love for other people - no competing
- They have a dramatic sense of self-confidence without arrogance

- Wants naturally decrease - no compulsions or musts
- They become free to pursue other interests

When needs are NOT met:
- Much time is wasted trying to get needs partially met
- One attracts needy people
- Frequent feelings of discouragement arise

What need do you have that is not being met?
- A place to be your authentic self
- An outlet to have fun and be playful
- Human touch
- Emotional support or a kind word daily
- Someone to tell you that "you can do it!"
- Other

_____
_____
_____
_____
_____
_____
_____
_____
_____
_____

Inspired Action and Results

THE CHALLENGE

Identify a personal need you want to meet fully:

_____
_____
_____
_____

Your plan to start meeting the need this week:

_____
_____
_____
_____

Authentic You

The Week in Action

Monday
Action Taken:

Hurdles Encountered:

The Plan to Move Forward Tomorrow:

Tuesday
Action Taken:

Hurdles Encountered:

The Plan to Move Forward Tomorrow:

Wednesday
Action Taken:

Hurdles Encountered:

The Plan to Move Forward Tomorrow:

Thursday
Action Taken:

Hurdles Encountered:

The Plan to Move Forward Tomorrow:

Friday
Action Taken:

Hurdles Encountered:

The Plan to Move Forward Tomorrow:

If you find yourself frequently "trying" to get someone to meet a need, reconsider your efforts. Experiment with a new way of thinking, doing or being to meet this need.

Inspired Action and Results

It's Already In You!

────────♦────────

Your unique greatness is already in you. It is revealed as you live in alignment with what is truly important to you, and what you are put on this earth to accomplish. It is in you and you hold the keys to unleash it.

What do you need to unlock and unleash your greatness?
- Inspiration
- An action plan
- Effective time management
- To honor your dream
- Increased personal limits to maximize your time and energy
- New skills
- Others

_____
_____
_____
_____
_____

I invite you to begin moving forward today to make your life shine as only you can!!

ACTION

One thing I will do today to begin unleashing my greatness:

_____
_____
_____
_____

Inspired Action and Results

THE WEEK IN ACTION

MONDAY
Action Taken:

Hurdles Encountered:

The Plan to Move Forward Tomorrow:

TUESDAY
Action Taken:

Hurdles Encountered:

The Plan to Move Forward Tomorrow:

WEDNESDAY
Action Taken:

Hurdles Encountered:

The Plan to Move Forward Tomorrow:

THURSDAY
Action Taken:

Hurdles Encountered:

The Plan to Move Forward Tomorrow:

FRIDAY
Action Taken:

Hurdles Encountered:

The Plan to Move Forward Tomorrow:

What's stopping you from unleashing your greatness?
Give yourself permission to fully express your greatness,
and take action!

"You are Here" - Right Where You Need to Be

Have you ever stopped to figure out your location at one of those maps in the big shopping malls? It always says "You are here." And from that point on it's easier to find your way to the various stores you want to visit.

Well, today I'd like to remind you that "you are here," and no matter what your life experiences may be, each one of them has brought you to this very moment. And in this moment, there is choice. You have been ushered right to the place where you need to be, in order to take your next step on the journey.

It's true that some of your life experiences are challenging right now, and it is also true that you are completely capable of handling them, and anything else that may come your way.

Today I challenge you to:

1. Trust your inner wisdom
2. Celebrate where you are in your life now

Inspired Action and Results

3. Commit to choices that support your greatness
4. Reach out and get the support needed to navigate it

ACTION

My "Next Step" to support living my best life this week:

_____
_____
_____
_____
_____

The Week in Action

Monday
Action Taken:

Hurdles Encountered:

The Plan to Move Forward Tomorrow:

Tuesday
Action Taken:

Hurdles Encountered:

The Plan to Move Forward Tomorrow:

Wednesday
Action Taken:

Hurdles Encountered:

The Plan to Move Forward Tomorrow:

Thursday
Action Taken:

Hurdles Encountered:

The Plan to Move Forward Tomorrow:

Friday
Action Taken:

Hurdles Encountered:

The Plan to Move Forward Tomorrow:

> Take a moment to pause. Acknowledge that you are right where you need to be. This will free you up to begin moving forward again.

Inspired Action and Results

The best way to predict the future is to create it.

Abraham Lincoln

A Winning Mindset

---◆---

Remember the once popular "magic eye" works of art? These were images that looked like nothing more than squiggly lines and dots of various colors all clumped together on a page. Only when the viewer would take time to focus, squint, look away and look again, could one expect to see something identifiable emerge.

Perspective shifts create not only new ways to look at the same old stuff, they also create new opportunities. These opportunities become available because what you see is what you can focus on, go after, and ultimately attain.

The real voyage of discovery consists not in seeking new landscapes, but in having new eyes. - Marcel Proust

Shift happens when you can see a difficult situation newly. Where there were once limited options, there emerges a path to new outcomes. Where there was previously frustration, there is now renewed energy to move forward. This shift comes when new information or ideas are presented and you discover a new way to see the old issue and create a new outcome.

Inspired Action and Results

A winning mindset is one that is able to see old situations newly. Remember that magic eye art? Some individuals have never been able to see the beauty that exists in the work, because they could never change their focus. This chapter invites you to view your life and your career in new ways that create a shift in perspective, a winning focus, and move you into action.

Bring It into Focus

---◆---

Recently I was out in nature, with all of its beauty, when I noticed something in the distance that looked like a dark shadow in a tree. It caught my interest – but I had no idea what it was. When I checked out the shadow through my binoculars, I was able to sharpen the focus and see what had captured my attention. What I nearly overlooked was actually a bald eagle sitting proudly in a distant tree. Like many things in life, it was something special that I wouldn't have seen if I hadn't taken the time, and used the tools to focus in on it.

What have you been "getting a glimpse of" in your life that is calling for your attention? It may be a very quiet request that keeps coming to your mind, a hope or a dream, or it could be the not-so-pleasant clamoring of a restless client or family member.

ACTION

Whatever it is that is calling for your attention, I'd like to invite you to bring it into focus. Take a few minutes now to clarify your area of focus, and make a plan for your next step.

Inspired Action and Results

What is calling for your attention?
_____
_____
_____
_____

What is your next step to start focusing on it?
_____
_____
_____
_____

Keep moving in the direction of your desired life.

A Winning Mindset

The Week in Action

Monday
Action Taken:

Hurdles Encountered:

The Plan to Move Forward Tomorrow:

Tuesday
Action Taken:

Hurdles Encountered:

The Plan to Move Forward Tomorrow:

Wednesday
Action Taken:

Hurdles Encountered:

The Plan to Move Forward Tomorrow:

Thursday
Action Taken:

Hurdles Encountered:

The Plan to Move Forward Tomorrow:

Friday
Action Taken:

Hurdles Encountered:

The Plan to Move Forward Tomorrow:

Sharpen the focus and take action this week!

Inspired Action and Results

Getting a Handle on "No"

---◆---

Occasionally, I use the microwave to boil a small amount of water in a cup just to warm the cup. As I hold the handle and begin to swirl the water around in the cup I see the power of the heat reflected in the rolling bubbles. It got me thinking about the skill involved in being able to roll the water around in the cup, while not letting it spill out onto my hand. All the while the boiling water moves ever-so-close to the top of the cup before tilting it in the other direction. This made me realize that the more I understand how water works, the more I can do with it.

What does that have to do with getting a handle on "no"? Some of us work very hard to stay as far away from that word as we can, for fear it will burn us - just like the boiling water. But the more we understand "no" – the way it works and what it might mean, the more likely we are to use it as a tool, rather than seeing it as a roadblock, to help reach goals. Let's take a look at what "no" may mean, depending on your understanding of it.

"No" as the decider:

Rejection

Feeling stuck

Hurt

Disappointment

Powerless

Out of options

Giving up

Losing

Finality

Embarrassment

"No" as a useful tool:

It becomes clarity for you It's time for a change

Not now, maybe later

A reminder to pause and rethink the approach

Safety/protection

A better alternative awaits you

A need to provide more information

Other possible meanings for you:

This week I challenge you to play with "no"! See what it might mean in your life as you skillfully learn to handle "no".

Inspired Action and Results

One area where getting a handle on "no" will help me:

_____
_____
_____
_____

One way I could interpret "no" so that it empowers me:

_____
_____
_____
_____

A Winning Mindset

The Week in Action

Monday

Action Taken:

Hurdles Encountered:

The Plan to Move Forward Tomorrow:

Tuesday

Action Taken:

Hurdles Encountered:

The Plan to Move Forward Tomorrow:

Wednesday

Action Taken:

Hurdles Encountered:

The Plan to Move Forward Tomorrow:

Thursday

Action Taken:

Hurdles Encountered:

The Plan to Move Forward Tomorrow:

Friday

Action Taken:

Hurdles Encountered:

The Plan to Move Forward Tomorrow:

Keep asking until you get at least 5 "No's"
you can play with each day this week!

Inspired Action and Results

Learning the Lesson To Advance

──────♦──────

Ever had to repeat a class because you didn't pass the test? "Passing the test" is really about mastering the material, or learning what it is you need to know to move forward.

What about your life today? What situations do you find that you are repeating again because you haven't "passed the test" to move on? It really seems to work that way. We get the same lesson disguised in different circumstances time and time again until we approach the test with a different strategy based on new learning and perspective.

So who or what is your course material today?

- Is it a co-worker you find challenging?
- An approach you are taking with your team?
- A belief you hold about yourself that keeps limiting you?

Doing something the same way and getting the same results is great if it is helping you on your path, but if the same behaviors are no longer serving you, it's time to use some new approaches to finally ace that test after all.

Use the skills you know you have, or ask for help from a trusted source.

Once you master the lesson, you will move on to the next level of your journey.

ACTION

One lesson I find myself facing over and over again:

_____
_____
_____
_____
_____

A new approach to get different results:

_____
_____
_____
_____
_____

Appreciate the lesson!

Inspired Action and Results

The Week in Action

Monday
Action Taken:

Hurdles Encountered:

The Plan to Move Forward Tomorrow:

Tuesday
Action Taken:

Hurdles Encountered:

The Plan to Move Forward Tomorrow:

Wednesday
Action Taken:

Hurdles Encountered:

The Plan to Move Forward Tomorrow:

Thursday
Action Taken:

Hurdles Encountered:

The Plan to Move Forward Tomorrow:

Friday
Action Taken:

Hurdles Encountered:

The Plan to Move Forward Tomorrow:

See your *learning challenge* as an opportunity to practice some new skills and gain some valuable experience. You've got this!

Opening Up Options

Ever feel stuck with limited options for making a decision? Are you finding yourself in an "either - or" situation, where neither option is an attractive solution? I recently worked with a client who thought she had to quit her job to start her new business. That kind of "either - or" thinking can keep competent, motivated people from moving out of a stuck place. Often the solution is someplace in the middle. The pressure of the situation frequently makes it even more challenging to see other alternatives. In this situation it turned out that my client could begin her new business parttime while she continued with her current position.

The next time you're feeling stuck, here are a few ideas to open up options...

- Let go of "either - or" thinking. If you feel stuck, ask yourself what your options are. When you find yourself thinking that you have to choose one or the other, see if you can come up with another option or two.

Inspired Action and Results

- Spend a few minutes free-writing about your situation. Let the thoughts flow from you - to the pen - to the paper with no edits or changes. Just letting thoughts flow can move you to a new perspective.

- Connect with a friend or coworker for a brainstorming session. When brainstorming, there is no right or wrong answer, and no criticism of the ideas. Often the goofiest ideas spur new thinking outside of the traditional box.

- Work with a coach who will assist you in tapping into your best ideas! You will receive the support needed to see new options that help you reach your goals.

ACTION

One area that I would like to open up options for myself:

_____
_____
_____
_____

One idea I will experiment with to open up new options:

_____
_____
_____
_____

The Week in Action

Monday
Action Taken:

Hurdles Encountered:

The Plan to Move Forward Tomorrow:

Tuesday
Action Taken:

Hurdles Encountered:

The Plan to Move Forward Tomorrow:

Wednesday
Action Taken:

Hurdles Encountered:

The Plan to Move Forward Tomorrow:

Thursday
Action Taken:

Hurdles Encountered:

The Plan to Move Forward Tomorrow:

Friday
Action Taken:

Hurdles Encountered:

The Plan to Move Forward Tomorrow:

Get a new perspective on the old situation, because often, what you see IS what you will get!

Inspired Action and Results

Releasing the Outcome

Ever find yourself "stuck" - unable to make the decisions or take the actions needed to get your life flowing effortlessly?

I affectionately described this condition as "frustrated perfectionism." Can't move forward, because it might not be just right. And can't go back- wards because you've already been there.

Now, please hear me say that thoughtful planning and listening to your intuition are important when deciding to move ahead. But if it's just a matter of entertaining fear, worry or anxiety, take action and release your attachment to the outcome. Put it out there, and know that however it turns out, it's okay.

Yes, it's possible that others may judge, and you may have to modify your plan along the way. You may also reach new heights you never thought possible!

Watch your spirit and your life soar. Release the outcome and begin moving in the direction of your desired outcomes.

ACTION

Where are you feeling stuck?

_____
_____
_____
_____
_____

What will you do differently to release the outcome and move forward?

_____
_____
_____
_____

Inspired Action and Results

The Week in Action

Monday
Action Taken:

Hurdles Encountered:

The Plan to Move Forward Tomorrow:

Tuesday
Action Taken:

Hurdles Encountered:

The Plan to Move Forward Tomorrow:

Wednesday
Action Taken:

Hurdles Encountered:

The Plan to Move Forward Tomorrow:

Thursday
Action Taken:

Hurdles Encountered:

The Plan to Move Forward Tomorrow:

Friday
Action Taken:

Hurdles Encountered:

The Plan to Move Forward Tomorrow:

Think newly, take action and create outcomes you really want! You are free to make adjustments along the way.

Rewrite Your Story!

We all create the stories about our lives based on our own perceptions of reality. Some of the stories have us playing the victim, others the hero. The next time you find yourself upset about something, take a moment to see what story you are telling yourself about the event, and your role in it. Are you showing up as powerful in your story? Or are you "being wronged" regularly?

Whatever your story is, you have the power to reshape your character and create a new story!

What new perspective can you give to your story? If you regularly show up as someone who is offended or made small in your story, what new thought would make the story different? Use your creativity and your insights to see yourself differently in your story this week. Adding humor, or even a new ending may create a new outcome for you. Practicing these tips can strengthen your role in this new story!

Inspired Action and Results

ACTION

One story you'd like to see newly this week:

_____
_____
_____
_____
_____

What new thought or action can you take to make it so:

_____
_____
_____
_____
_____

The Week in Action

Monday
Action Taken:

Hurdles Encountered:

The Plan to Move Forward Tomorrow:

Tuesday
Action Taken:

Hurdles Encountered:

The Plan to Move Forward Tomorrow:

Wednesday
Action Taken:

Hurdles Encountered:

The Plan to Move Forward Tomorrow:

Thursday
Action Taken:

Hurdles Encountered:

The Plan to Move Forward Tomorrow:

Friday
Action Taken:

Hurdles Encountered:

The Plan to Move Forward Tomorrow:

Practicing the insights you gain here will strengthen your new role in your story!

Inspired Action and Results

The Value of the Stinky Stuff

For those of you who have lived near a farm, or have planted a garden using fertilizer, you probably know what fertilizer is, and how offensive it smells - pretty stinky. Yet that stinky stuff is required to get the maximum yield on crops that have been planted. Without fertilizer, you can't begin to get those results.

Today I invite you to see your "failures" as the stinky stuff - fertilizer that will increase your results both in work and in life. And maybe failure is just a perspective, and when you shift your perspective, your failures become experiences, or fertilizer, to make your life that much richer and you that much wiser.

My challenge to you is to reframe that experience as fertilizer growing you on your path to greatness!

Know that prosperity will emerge from this experience. As we know from planting, there is an incubation period before the actual results are seen. It may take some time for the growth to become evident. Trust the process – it is good.

ACTION

What experience has felt like failure for you recently?

_____
_____
_____
_____
_____

How can this experience, like fertilizer, help you achieve your goals?

_____
_____
_____
_____
_____

Inspired Action and Results

The Week in Action

Monday
Action Taken:

Hurdles Encountered:

The Plan to Move Forward Tomorrow:

Tuesday
Action Taken:

Hurdles Encountered:

The Plan to Move Forward Tomorrow:

Wednesday
Action Taken:

Hurdles Encountered:

The Plan to Move Forward Tomorrow:

Thursday
Action Taken:

Hurdles Encountered:

The Plan to Move Forward Tomorrow:

Friday
Action Taken:

Hurdles Encountered:

The Plan to Move Forward Tomorrow:

See failure as a *learning* opportunity. **FAIL** - **F**irst **A**ttempt **I**n **L**earning.

What You Resist Will Persist

Ever find yourself arguing with reality - thinking that your circumstances should be different than they are? For example....

- I shouldn't have to work so hard
- My partner shouldn't criticize me
- My kids ought to do something when I ask

When we resist the way things are currently by thinking that they should be different, we are judging our present reality - and fighting against it.

It's almost like thrashing around in a vast ocean when you don't know how to swim. Pretty pointless. As long as you keep resisting it, it keeps getting the best of you.

I had the pleasure of working with a highly motivated advisor who wanted to lose weight. Most of the clothes in her closet no longer fit her well, yet she kept saving them because she thought she would lose weight someday. When she accepted the fact that she no longer fit into most of her clothing, she decided to donate

Inspired Action and Results

it. In just a few months she decided it was time to consult with a nutritionist and began eating and moving in a way that supported her weight loss. After accepting the fact of her current reality, she was somehow freed up and inspired to change it.

Author Byron Katie teaches that one key to moving the circumstance forward is first accepting what *is*[15]. Without judging it, fighting it, or being angry at yourself, state your concern honestly, and accept it. This doesn't mean you have to let it stay that way forever. In fact, after deciding to accept (and no longer resist) your current situation, you can then make a clear decision to:

1. Continue with your reality as it is and learn to enjoy it

2. Continue with your reality as it is and be unhappy, or angry, or

3. Make a plan to begin changing whatever it is you initially found yourself resisting (optimistically - free of judgment.)

ACTION

Identify one thing you are currently resisting:

_____
_____
_____
_____
_____

A Winning Mindset

How you will accept it and move forward this week:

_____
_____
_____
_____
_____

Inspired Action and Results

The Week in Action

Monday
Action Taken:

Hurdles Encountered:

The Plan to Move Forward Tomorrow:

Tuesday
Action Taken:

Hurdles Encountered:

The Plan to Move Forward Tomorrow:

Wednesday
Action Taken:

Hurdles Encountered:

The Plan to Move Forward Tomorrow:

Thursday
Action Taken:

Hurdles Encountered:

The Plan to Move Forward Tomorrow:

Friday
Action Taken:

Hurdles Encountered:

The Plan to Move Forward Tomorrow:

Accept what you are resisting by verbally stating: "Yes, it has been true that _____ (insert your concern), and now I am accepting it as so." You may notice that you feel differently about the situation. It may bring up feelings, or new ideas. Then you can make your next step or plan.

The Re-think Process

I recently worked with an executive who was hesitant to confront one of his team members due to concern that she would be offended by the concern. We spent a few minutes discussing the situation and I invited him to look at the interaction as a development opportunity. As he began to see this process as part of his role, and his commitment to develop each of his team members, the possibilities for the conversation became much more attractive and therefore much more doable.

Albert Einstein, 1921 Nobel Prize winner for Physics, stated that; "No problem can be solved from the same level of consciousness that created it." Today I invite you to gain a new view on a tough situation. Move your thinking to a different level through this quick re-think process.

The Re-think Process:

1. Identify one thing in your life that you would currently describe as a problem.

Inspired Action and Results

2. Now take a minute to really play with this situation, re-thinking it as each the following:

   A. a challenge to overcome

   B. an opportunity to embrace

   C. a gift to you

Tip: If you normally sit while thinking, stand up or walk around. Even consider dancing, playing music or running while you think.

Notice what happens to your thoughts and emotions when you view the problem as a challenge, an opportunity or a gift.

ACTION

One problem I will use the Re-think process on today:

_____
_____
_____
_____

What I notice as I consider this problem as a challenge, an opportunity and a gift:

_____
_____
_____
_____

The Week in Action

Monday
Action Taken:

Hurdles Encountered:

The Plan to Move Forward Tomorrow:

Tuesday
Action Taken:

Hurdles Encountered:

The Plan to Move Forward Tomorrow:

Wednesday
Action Taken:

Hurdles Encountered:

The Plan to Move Forward Tomorrow:

Thursday
Action Taken:

Hurdles Encountered:

The Plan to Move Forward Tomorrow:

Friday
Action Taken:

Hurdles Encountered:

The Plan to Move Forward Tomorrow:

The problem isn't the problem. Frequently it's the thinking about the problem, or even labeling it as a problem, that holds us back.- Rachelle

Reset Your Default

For many years I didn't know that I could reset my default setting for the text font on my email. The default setting had been a Times New Roman font and I really prefer Arial, so I was pleased to learn that I could actually reset the default to a font of my choosing.

This led me to think about the ways in which we react to situations in life. We tend to respond with our default setting based on our usual thoughts and emotions. For instance, if you see that your annual productivity and revenue is down, you may react with feelings of anxiety or fear. And that would be really natural. But how about the possibility of adjusting your default setting based on information you have, such as knowing that your skillset and strengths would work in other environments, and that no matter what happens, you can use this experience as learning for your next step in your career.

Often, we give ourselves a limiting message based on our default setting, without realizing that the way we are thinking about the situation causes our emotional response, and frequently ends up impacting our actual results. So this week I invite you to create a new default setting!

One situation where your "default response" is limiting your joy or success:

_____
_____
_____
_____
_____

A more beneficial default setting you can put in its place:

_____
_____
_____
_____

Inspired Action and Results

The Week in Action

Monday

Action Taken:

Hurdles Encountered:

The Plan to Move Forward Tomorrow:

Tuesday

Action Taken:

Hurdles Encountered:

The Plan to Move Forward Tomorrow:

Wednesday

Action Taken:

Hurdles Encountered:

The Plan to Move Forward Tomorrow:

Thursday

Action Taken:

Hurdles Encountered:

The Plan to Move Forward Tomorrow:

Friday

Action Taken:

Hurdles Encountered:

The Plan to Move Forward Tomorrow:

Notice how your week unfolds after resetting your default response! Remember, it will take conscious practice to choose your new, preferred default mode. If you would like support to create a new default setting, contact me for a complimentary conversation!

Recharge in 59 seconds!

If you could refocus and center yourself in 59 seconds to be at your best, would you?

Today I challenge you to begin practicing the 59 second recharge!

1. Start in a seated position with both feet flat on the ground.

2. Close your eyes and take a deep, cleansing breath, slowly inhaling through your nose and then exhaling slowly through your mouth (repeat if needed!)

3. Shift your focus to see your blessings floating across a clear blue sky as you breathe calmly and slowly. See people, places, your health, a kind act, your intelligence, a beautiful painting, the color of grass, the creative ideas you have, etc., all floating by like a great appreciation movie rolling across a beautiful sky.

4. After a few seconds, take another deep breath, knowing that your life is a gift.

Inspired Action and Results

You have completed the recharge. Keep making it a great day!

Five things you will put in your appreciation movie clip today:

1.

2.

3.

4.

5.

The Week in Action

Monday
Action Taken:

Hurdles Encountered:

The Plan to Move Forward Tomorrow:

Tuesday
Action Taken:

Hurdles Encountered:

The Plan to Move Forward Tomorrow:

Wednesday
Action Taken:

Hurdles Encountered:

The Plan to Move Forward Tomorrow:

Thursday
Action Taken:

Hurdles Encountered:

The Plan to Move Forward Tomorrow:

Friday
Action Taken:

Hurdles Encountered:

The Plan to Move Forward Tomorrow:

Invest 59 seconds to recharge daily when you need it. How about right before/after a challenging appointment, or before your first appointment each day!

Inspired Action and Results

Lighten Your Luggage!

Recently I took a trip that required carrying some heavy luggage, as well as toting a computer bag and a large purse to sustain me for ten days out of town. I wondered if I really needed all of the products, clothing, etc. that were weighing me down. As usual, at the end of the trip there were several items I never used.

I thought about how much lighter my load may have been if I had courageously released some of the items I was taking on the trip.

This led me to wonder about the many thoughts we "pack and carry" that keep us from experiencing our desired life. It may be a limiting belief about our abilities, a fear about money, or something else.

This week, I invite you to try the following to lighten your luggage:

1. Identify a thought or belief that holds you back
2. Imagine that you are carrying it in a (big) piece of luggage.

3. When you get ready to step into a new experience, make a conscious decision to lighten up your emotional load and leave your "baggage" (or belief) at the door. Just set it down and leave it. (You can pick it up again if you ever need it.)

4. Pick up a new, lighter belief that serves you better, such as "I am enough to do this project well" or "I have the resources at my disposal to make this happen!"

Today I will leave this baggage behind:

_____
_____
_____
_____

The new lighter, belief I will take with me:

_____
_____
_____
_____

Inspired Action and Results

The Week in Action

Monday
Action Taken:

Hurdles Encountered:

The Plan to Move Forward Tomorrow:

Tuesday
Action Taken:

Hurdles Encountered:

The Plan to Move Forward Tomorrow:

Wednesday
Action Taken:

Hurdles Encountered:

The Plan to Move Forward Tomorrow:

Thursday
Action Taken:

Hurdles Encountered:

The Plan to Move Forward Tomorrow:

Friday
Action Taken:

Hurdles Encountered:

The Plan to Move Forward Tomorrow:

Trust that whatever remains with you is everything needed to step fully into your greatest life!

Just Business

Upon hearing the saying, "it's just business" I am reminded of a few points about being in business and what that saying means:

1. Use your objectivity - Don't take it personally when something happens in a business relationship. Use it as information to make adjustments to your course of action.

2. Lighten up - Enjoy your work and don't take it, or yourself, too seriously. Let your work be a source of fulfillment.

3. Have multiple points of joy in your life - Take time for a life outside of your work so that not all of your self-worth & joy is tied up in your career. It's often those other points of joy that energize and recharge us to get back to the work feeling renewed.

4. Stay sharp in your industry - Ongoing training and information gathering will give you valuable insight into the direction to move before the rest of the pack notices.

Inspired Action and Results

5. Create a great success community - Connect with other professionals for advice and referrals. Notice how the concept of "just business" can take on new and powerful dimensions when you are connected to others in your business community.

ACTION

One thing I will do this week to practice the concept of it's just business.

_____
_____
_____
_____
_____

The Week in Action

Monday
Action Taken:

Hurdles Encountered:

The Plan to Move Forward Tomorrow:

Tuesday
Action Taken:

Hurdles Encountered:

The Plan to Move Forward Tomorrow:

Wednesday
Action Taken:

Hurdles Encountered:

The Plan to Move Forward Tomorrow:

Thursday
Action Taken:

Hurdles Encountered:

The Plan to Move Forward Tomorrow:

Friday
Action Taken:

Hurdles Encountered:

The Plan to Move Forward Tomorrow:

Notice one way you can lighten up and enjoy your work each day this week!

Inspired Action and Results

Are You At Your Cruising Altitude?

───────♦───────

When an airplane takes off, it uses four to five times more fuel (energy) than it does at its "cruising altitude." That led me to think about making changes in life. When we set out to do something new – grow a business, have a child, end a relationship, or move, just to name a few, it tends to take much more energy than normal, everyday life. Even when we strive to change our thinking, it can be like moving the airplane to a new altitude, with habitual thinking of the past sometimes holding us like the power of gravity!

Take a moment to see where you are in your own life. Are you giving yourself the necessary support, energy, kindness and resources to get back to your cruising altitude? Know that you will require more time, attention and support during these times of transition. Give yourself some grace, along with the energy needed, and you will get you back to your cruising altitude once again!

ACTION

One area of your life where you are using energy due to a transition:

_____
_____
_____
_____

Support you need to get back to cruising altitude:

_____
_____
_____
_____

How you will get that support this week:

_____
_____
_____
_____

Inspired Action and Results

The Week in Action

Monday

Action Taken:

Hurdles Encountered:

The Plan to Move Forward Tomorrow:

Tuesday

Action Taken:

Hurdles Encountered:

The Plan to Move Forward Tomorrow:

Wednesday

Action Taken:

Hurdles Encountered:

The Plan to Move Forward Tomorrow:

Thursday

Action Taken:

Hurdles Encountered:

The Plan to Move Forward Tomorrow:

Friday

Action Taken:

Hurdles Encountered:

The Plan to Move Forward Tomorrow:

Invest your energy in what is important to you. Surround yourself with people who energize you, and limit your time with the rest.

A Winning Mindset

Honoring the Duck that Lays the Golden Eggs

◆

We've all heard the story of the goose that laid the golden eggs, but Daniel Amos, CEO of AFLAC insurance found his "goose" in the form of a tenacious and irritable quacking duck - the AFLAC duck. Using the duck for marketing was a gamble, yet after test markets gave the duck a "thumbs up," Dan decided to go for it. And his duck layed many a golden eggs in the form of name recognition and success for the AFLAC company.[18]

In honor of it's importance, Dan insisted that no duck-related foods be served at any of his company functions. No duck pate', no crispy duck, no duck soup, no Peking duck, and no duck a' la Orange. The duck earned a place of honor in the AFLAC company.

In your organization, what has proven to be your "golden duck?" Is it:

- A referral source that keeps business coming in regularly?

Inspired Action and Results

- Keeping your health in top shape so you can run it effectively?
- A partner who is there to hear you and cheer you on the journey?
- A mentor or coach who challenges you to stay focused and be your best?
- Incredible client service?
- A great office in the right location for you?
- A top performing team member?

Whatever your "golden duck" is, take some time this week to determine how you can best honor it so that it keeps delivering in the way that supports your success.

My organization's golden duck:

ACTION

How I will honor it:

_____
_____
_____
_____
_____

A Winning Mindset

The Week in Action

Monday
Action Taken:

Hurdles Encountered:

The Plan to Move Forward Tomorrow:

Tuesday
Action Taken:

Hurdles Encountered:

The Plan to Move Forward Tomorrow:

Wednesday
Action Taken:

Hurdles Encountered:

The Plan to Move Forward Tomorrow:

Thursday
Action Taken:

Hurdles Encountered:

The Plan to Move Forward Tomorrow:

Friday
Action Taken:

Hurdles Encountered:

The Plan to Move Forward Tomorrow:

Get clear on what (or who) is your "golden duck" this week. Take action to honor and appreciate their contributions to your success.

Inspired Action and Results

Live Like You Mean It

When you hear the phrase, "live like you mean it" what comes up for you? For some it may be taking an adventure vacation, for another it may be increasing business or taking a leadership role in making the community better. And yet for others it may mean something as simple as showing up 10 minutes early for all appointments.

What about you? What is one thing that would really reflect a life of living like you mean it?

_____
_____
_____
_____
_____

This week I invite you to live like you mean it!

ACTION

One thing I commit to in my quest to live like I mean it:

_____
_____
_____
_____

Inspired Action and Results

The Week in Action

Monday
Action Taken:

Hurdles Encountered:

The Plan to Move Forward Tomorrow:

Tuesday
Action Taken:

Hurdles Encountered:

The Plan to Move Forward Tomorrow:

Wednesday
Action Taken:

Hurdles Encountered:

The Plan to Move Forward Tomorrow:

Thursday
Action Taken:

Hurdles Encountered:

The Plan to Move Forward Tomorrow:

Friday
Action Taken:

Hurdles Encountered:

The Plan to Move Forward Tomorrow:

Take specific action each day this week to live like you mean it!

A Winning Mindset

Lucky 13

When you think of the number 13, do you think of "lucky"? Traditionally, that number has represented "bad luck" for those who believe there really is such a thing. You may notice that elevators do not have a 13 because often buildings skip the 13th floor due to the superstitious meaning. Well, I was born on the 13th, so for me that number means celebration and good cheer.

The question this brings me to: Is there a particular challenge in your life that you've been viewing as a traditional, superstitious 13? If so, can you take something that seems like a "bad situation" and give it new meaning? Generally when we look at our tough experiences in hindsight, we find that they provided a time of growth and learning that eventually ushered us into a new place in life. Today I invite you to begin seeing your own "13" as lucky!

Inspired Action and Results

ACTION

What situation has been showing up as the "13" in your life?

_____
_____
_____
_____

What new meaning could you give that situation in order to turn it into something "Lucky?"

_____
_____
_____
_____

THE WEEK IN ACTION

MONDAY
Action Taken:

Hurdles Encountered:

The Plan to Move Forward Tomorrow:

TUESDAY
Action Taken:

Hurdles Encountered:

The Plan to Move Forward Tomorrow:

WEDNESDAY
Action Taken:

Hurdles Encountered:

The Plan to Move Forward Tomorrow:

THURSDAY
Action Taken:

Hurdles Encountered:

The Plan to Move Forward Tomorrow:

FRIDAY
Action Taken:

Hurdles Encountered:

The Plan to Move Forward Tomorrow:

You will often feel "Lucky" when you see your life through eyes of gratitude! Develop a daily practice of gratitude, thanking God for ALL things.

Practice Makes Perfect

We've all heard the saying, "practice makes perfect." And as kids, that may have meant something like hearing a parent say, "Get back to the piano and practice!"

In 2006 Fortune magazine reported on "What it takes to be great." [19]

Is it talent? Do you have to be born with a golf club in your hand to become a Tiger Woods? Well, according to the Fortune article, the LACK of natural talent is irrelevant to great success. What they found is that consistent, focused, and relentless practice is the predictor of future success! So while it may be true that a basketball player has an advantage if he is very tall, you can become very successful without that natural advantage. Take retired NBA player Spud Webb, who, at 5'6" won the NBA Slam Dunk contest in 1986. He is one of many who committed to his passion and showed us that "you don't have to be born with it all to be successful at it!"

A Winning Mindset

What is it that you are working to accomplish this year - in your career, relationships or life overall? Whatever it is, consider how focused practice could help you create the results you really want, and get started today!

ACTION

One thing I've been working to accomplish this year:

_____
_____
_____
_____
_____

What I can begin doing (practicing) to make it happen:

_____
_____
_____
_____
_____

Inspired Action and Results

The Week in Action

Monday

Action Taken:

Hurdles Encountered:

The Plan to Move Forward Tomorrow:

Tuesday

Action Taken:

Hurdles Encountered:

The Plan to Move Forward Tomorrow:

Wednesday

Action Taken:

Hurdles Encountered:

The Plan to Move Forward Tomorrow:

Thursday

Action Taken:

Hurdles Encountered:

The Plan to Move Forward Tomorrow:

Friday

Action Taken:

Hurdles Encountered:

The Plan to Move Forward Tomorrow:

> Discipline is doing what you want to do,
> even when you don't want to do it!

What's in Your Bucket?

A bucket can only hold so much water. If you let stale water collect in a bucket, soon there is no room for fresh water. And even if you add fresh water, it is quickly contaminated by the stale stuff. Same concept with your life. When you keep stale and draining situations filling your life, there is no room for something fresh.

By releasing the stale and draining influences in your life, you create a space for something new and fresh that works for you.

Today I challenge you to make a list of the top 5 things in your bucket (personal or professional) that you really don't want to keep in there. Then pick one and design a way to remove it. Next week do the same. In 5 weeks you will have taken a number of things out of your bucket, creating space for the fresh, new life you prefer to live.

TIP: Be selective when you bring "fresh water" into your bucket. Whatever it is, make sure that it resonates with you before allowing it in.

Inspired Action and Results

ACTION

The top 5 things I want to remove from my bucket:

1.

2.

3.

4.

5.

This week I will start with:

_____
_____
_____
_____
_____

A Winning Mindset

The Week in Action

Monday
Action Taken:

Hurdles Encountered:

The Plan to Move Forward Tomorrow:

Tuesday
Action Taken:

Hurdles Encountered:

The Plan to Move Forward Tomorrow:

Wednesday
Action Taken:

Hurdles Encountered:

The Plan to Move Forward Tomorrow:

Thursday
Action Taken:

Hurdles Encountered:

The Plan to Move Forward Tomorrow:

Friday
Action Taken:

Hurdles Encountered:

The Plan to Move Forward Tomorrow:

Begin to release the stale and draining influences. How can you selectively fill your bucket with fresh energy and perspective this week? It may take time. That's okay. Start today.

Comfort and Courage for the Soul

---◆---

Just as there are times in life when we may require time and rest to restore physical health, there are also times in life when the soul needs extra care and encouragement.

In those times, I frequently drawn strength from my faith in a living God and in the inspired Word. Here are a few of my favorite passages. They are words of hope to remind me that ultimately, God's got this, and that it will all be well with my soul. I hope you find comfort in these words as well.

Future Plans

For I know the plans I have for you, says the Lord. Plans to prosper you, not to harm you. Plans to give you a hope and a future.

Jeremiah 29:11

Peace

You, Lord, will keep in perfect peace all who trust in you, all whose thoughts are fixed on you.

Isaiah 26:3

Fear

For God has not given us a spirit of fear, but of power, and of love, and of a sound mind.

II Timothy 1:7

Hope

They that hope in the Lord will renew their strength. They will soar with wings of eagles. They will run and not grow weary. They will walk and not faint.

Isaiah 40:31

A Blessing to Share

May the Lord bless you and keep you. May the Lord make His face to shine upon you and be gracious to you; the Lord turn his face toward you, and give you peace.

Numbers 6:24-26

References

1. Sinek, S. (2011) Start With Why. Portfolio Publishing.

2. Tracy, Brian (2017) Eat that Frog! Third edition. (Berrett-Koehler Publishers, Inc.)

3. Johnson, S. (1998) Who moved my cheese? New York: Putnam.

4. Olson, J. and Mann, J.D. (2005) The Slight Edge. Austin, Texas: Greenleaf Book Group Press

5. Bryant, L.K. (2005) Trust Yourself to Transform Your Body: A Woman's Guide to Health and Weight Loss Without Diets. Crimson Leaf Publishing.

6. Collins, J. C. (2001). Good to great: Why some companies make the leap... and others don't. New York, NY: HarperBusiness.

7. Kashyap, V.(2019, May 20) Effective Communication in the Workplace: How and Why? Employee Engagement. HR Technologist. https://www.hrtechnologist.com/articles/employee-

engagement/effective-communication-in-the-workplace-how-and-why/

8. Blanchard, K. and McBride, M. (2003) The One-Minute Apology. Harper Collins (New York, NY)

9. Lyon, L. (2009, June 24) A Quick Tip For Improving Relationships -Using Positive Psychology in your Relationships. U.S. News and World Report

10. Bailey, K. and Leland, K. (2006) Customer Service For Dummies 3rd Edition. Wiley Publishing

11. Thorndike, E. (1932) The Fundamentals of Learning. New York: Teachers College Press.

12. Anderson, M. and Parker, S. (2006) The Extra Degree. Simple Truths Press.

13. Wright Brothers Aero plane Company. (2013) https://wrightbros.org/History_Wing/Wright_Story/Inventing_the_Air-plane/Not_Within_A_Thousand_Years/Not_Within_A_Thousand_Years.htm

14. Williamson, M. (1996) A Return to Love: Reflections on the Principles of "A Course in Miracles". Harper One Publishers.

15. Harvard Medical School. (2019, July 29) Five Ways to de-stress and help your heart. Harvard Health Publishing. https://www.health.harvard.edu/heart-health/5-ways-to-de-stress-and-help-your-heart

16. Buckingham, M and Clifton, O. Ph.D. (2001) Now Discover Your Strengths. The Free Press.

17. Katie, B. and Mitchell, S. (2003) Loving What Is. Three Rivers Press.

18. The Business Journals (2020, October 13) Strategies from Aflac's origins provide insights for business innovators today. Atlanta Business Chronicle. https://www.bizjournals.com/atlanta/news/2020/10/13/strate-gies-from-aflac-s-origins-provide-insights-f.html

19. Fortune Magazine (2006, October 19) What it takes to be great. Geoffrey Colvin https://archive.fortune.com/magazines/fortune/fortune_archive/2006/10/30/8391794/index.htm

ASK!

---◆---

As I take steps to grow and make changes in my own life, and as I challenge clients to take their next steps, I am keenly aware of the need to ask for what is needed. Yet time and time again, people aren't asking. Maybe they are afraid to hear the answer.

"Asking" is like using a muscle. At first it is difficult, and doesn't always get you your desired results. But with practice you get better and better at it, feeling stronger each time you ask. And even when the answer is no, it becomes a point of clarity for future direction, rather than something that disappoints or discourages.

Tips for asking:

1. Practice - Commit to asking for things just to get practice. Ask for samples at the store, ask for a discount on your phone service, ask your team to do something extra this week. Ask your clients for referrals. ASK, ASK, ASK!!!

2. Be Clear and Confident - Know what you want and state it Confidently. If you want to collaborate with another professional to increase both of your referrals, express your idea with conviction that it would benefit both of you!

3. Take it lightly - If someone says "NO" - roll with it. Don't take it personally. We know that "No" can mean various things – not now, call in 6 months, I don't have the bandwidth currently, etc. Celebrate honesty and clarity – and circle back to them when the time seems right.

4. Trust that people you ask are able to answer you honestly and set their own limits. You do your work (ask) and let them do their work (answer).

This week I invite you to ASK for what you need.

One thing I will ask for this week:

_____
_____
_____
_____
_____

Three ways I will keep practicing my ask this week:

1.

2.

3.

Your Invitation to Inspired Action and Results

Make it a year to remember! Take an energized journey through 52 weeks of coaching. Individually, or with your team, create new results and new joy, with one year of weekly coaching. See what you can create in your career, with your personal wellness, in relationships and in your life! You choose the focus. We work together to create the results.

Contact Rachelle for a customized plan to inspire and challenge you in meeting and exceeding your desired outcomes. Why wait - start today!

About Rachelle

Rachelle is a Professional Certified Coach with the International Coaching Federation and a licensed clinical psychotherapist. Her greatest joy is helping individuals stretch fully into the person they are designed to become. She has successfully led individuals and teams through transitions, and works to strengthen engagement in business and in life. Rachelle has served as an ICF Charter Chapter board member for over a decade, in multiple roles, and is past president of the ICF Heartland Charter Chapter, and past president the ICF Arizona Charter Chapter.

Rachelle resides in Kansas City, MO with her family. She finds joy in nature, time with friends and family, sunsets, and kicking up her heels with a ballroom dance lesson. Rachelle can be reached for a coaching consultation at

www.CoachRachelle.com.

www.ingramcontent.com/pod-product-compliance
Lightning Source LLC
Chambersburg PA
CBHW060831220526
45466CB00003B/1059